We Are Here

Love Never Dies

Jane Smith Bernhardt

Burnham Press

LCCN: 2008930615
ISBN-13: 978-0-615-34131-6

Design by Kat Mack
www.melodicadesign.com

Typeset in Century Schoolbook
1 2 3 4 5 6 7 8 9 0

"The last enemy to be destroyed is death."

1 Corinthians 15:26
(New Testament: Revised Standard Version)

"So this is death! ... Life separated by density— that is all!"

(Testimony of Light, the words of Sr. Francis Banks, in afterlife, received by Helen Greaves.)

Table of Contents

FOREWORD

There are things which happen in our lives that can only be understood within the realm of the miraculous. We simply have no rational explanation for these moments where the impossible interrupts our known universe. Now we believe that the world is round and revolves around the sun. But there was a time when such notions were regarded as mad impossibilities. This book holds an impossible story in which miracles of forgiveness and transformation arrive from beyond life. I cannot blame you if you find it unbelievable: I would not have believed it myself three years ago. But suppose for a moment it isn't madness.

Suppose that a man can accompany his widow through her final earthly passage from the other side of death. Suppose that another man while in a coma can meet spiritual helpers who illuminate a realm of forgiveness and hope so powerful that he returns transformed to heal his family before leaving his earthly life. What would these possibilities mean to our lives, and even our world? That we are eternal souls on a mortal journey, that life and love and healing are infinite ... that eternal joy is each person's birthright and destiny. I ask you to take this unbelievable journey with me. Because it happened, and I was gifted to be a messenger of spiritual guidance that is remarkably beautiful and wise.

In addition to being a wife and the mother of three grown children and step-mother to three more wonderful young people, I am a free-lance artist and actress. I paint portraits, teach, and perform original dramatic pieces. I have also been a spiritual seeker. Ten years ago I completed a two-year program with the Guild for Spiritual Guidance and have infused the desire for social healing into my visual art and performance.

I have spent large portions of my life waiting on inspiration. What I have come to understand is that some of the projects that feel the most meaningful require so much effort that they can only be accomplished with support from what I call Spirit. Sometimes I've named this spirit God, and sometimes I've thought of it as deep inner guidance. These days I have the sense that there are spirit friends who help me on my journey.

The first truly demanding creative task I undertook was during the Cold War. In my deep desire to help my young children grow up in a world free of the threat of nuclear annihilation, I prayerfully asked what I could do to help bridge the fearsome East/West divide. In the early 1980's I read an article about a Russian prisoner in Germany during the Second World War who had drawn portraits of his captors, creating delicate renderings of the individual humanity of these "enemies." In that moment my calling was born: I would journey to the Soviet Union to draw charcoal portraits of enemy faces to bring back to the US for a traveling exhibit.

Funds had to be raised, I needed my family's support, and I struggled with great inner doubt, but the sense of calling sustained me, and the exhibit was a success. It was warmly received in schools, libraries, churches and galleries.

In subsequent years I created original dramatic productions and three more thematic art exhibits. I adapted the letters and diaries of the Holocaust victim Etty Hillesum and performed them as a solo piece in many parts of the United States and Europe. I was privileged to speak Etty's inspiring words of passion and faith from a small stage at the place of her death, Auschwitz Concentration Camp in Poland.

In August of 2003, driven by my concern over a U.S. plan to create a new generation of "mini nukes" ranging from one-third to three times the size of the nuclear bomb dropped on Hiroshima in 1945, I traveled to Hiroshima to create a series of collage portraits and stories of some of the remaining survivors, the "Hibakusha." With the help of several creative colleagues, I wove these pieces into a multi-media performance.

Each time my enormous creative effort would be followed by a long period of inactivity, the fallow time when there was no inspiration in sight. This fallow time can be very disturbing to one who is invested in the process and fruit of her work. For me, the times of waiting are often haunting, and I yearn for the next great undertaking, a sense of inadequacy gnawing at my soul. After the great effort of the Hibakusha Peace Project, I expected to wait for several months and then begin to feel the seeds of new direction.

In this time I was learning about meditation from a gentle teacher who made the process of sitting in stillness both safe and inviting. I began to welcome the empty space where I could slowly disengage from mental agenda or expectation. I even began to have warm feelings and sudden unbidden insights which I would record in my journal as they came. Still I waited for the next great project.

In this waiting I would cry out to the silence: "What next? What am I supposed to do? Where is my life's direction?" And the questions would be met with more silence. At last I began to understand that silence was itself the answer: My direction was to wait. And so I tried to honor this quiet time more deliberately. Sitting comfortably, preferably with a cup of tea and my cat in my lap, I would be quiet.

I think of a heron, stick-still in shallow water, whose patience is sometimes rewarded with a succulent catch. After waiting until the buzzing thoughts had tired of themselves, sometimes I could sense a loving presence nearby. Listening with my heart, I seemed to feel a message. I learned that if I could write as I received these thoughts they often continued unedited by my own mind. And at last I began to see this was my next great project, to receive the messages of the loving spirit companions who speak to my waiting heart.

One of the first of these messages came while I was preparing an address to the 9/11 Families for Peaceful Tomorrows during their 2004 peace-walk. As I waited in silence trying to imagine a speech worthy of this gathering, the beautiful words began to articulate themselves and I simply wrote. The message was surprisingly moving and not at all the motivational talk I'd presumed the occasion warranted. It was an invitation really, to open and grieve and understand the gift of the "wounded healer" to our wounded earth.

As it turned out, on the stifling August day of our gathering these peace pilgrims were exhausted from the effort of their walk between the Democratic and Republican political conventions in Boston and New York, hauling a mammoth marker in memory of the innocents who have died in war. They didn't need an education on disarmament: What they needed was an invitation to be deeply real and honest with one another in our intimate circle. It was a sacred gathering. For me, it was an early experiment in trusting a spiritual message for which I could not verify a source.

Two more years of waiting and listening were perhaps preparation for a new calling: A journey through the veil of death. At the beginning of the journey I only imagined the possibility that the dead can communicate with the living. I was new to the notion of "channeling" spiritual messages. In a sense this one year was a crash course in the continuing nature of life and in the awesome power of Love.

In a strange way this book about the death of my father and step-mother and my children's father is the most joyful thing I have ever done. Along with exhausting waves of grief, there were exhilarating revelations whose white light has blasted though my prior conceptions of death as ending and life itself as finite.

Imagine knowing that your loved ones are still present and available after death and that you are at all times surrounded by a host of spiritual and ancestral helpers.

Imagine believing that everything is made up of the unfolding creative energy of Love: all forgiving, all healing ... through death and beyond.

Imagine that all things are possible in Love.

Jane Smith Bernhardt
May 2009

1: BEGINNING

Twenty years ago I asked my father, Harry Lee Smith, to help me with my fear of death. I had faith in the omnipresence of God — or Loving Spirit — but I could not sincerely believe that conscious life survives the body's death. My dad, in one of our long bi-coastal phone calls, said: "I don't doubt it at all." He sent me Dr. Raymond Moody's *Life After Life*, in which a medical doctor chronicles studies of patients' near-death experiences. This began a wonderful correspondence as we shared books and meditations in our quest for deeper understanding of the divine. He introduced me to the teachings of Yogananda, an Indian yogi he admired, and I sent him Thomas Merton and Thich Nhat Hanh. Once or twice we even imagined the possibility of our conversations continuing after he had passed on beyond death.

On November fifth of 2006, my eldest sister Carol called to say that our father had died in the night. We were shocked, as all year our attention had been focused on his bed-bound wife Angelika's severe health crises. In spite of his own fatigue at age 87, he had been her care-giver.

Although my father had been seeking spiritual growth for many years and had no doubt about the eternal destiny of his spirit, I was devastated by this news: It was one thing to speak of the immortal soul, and quite another to contemplate a world without my father's counsel and presence.

There had been a newness to the spiritual curiosity of his late years, a child-like enthusiasm for his spiritual awakening as he deliberately prepared himself for the adventure he anticipated would follow this life. And even as I reeled from the sudden realization that I would never again see his face or hear his voice on the phone, I was grateful for the manner of his passing because it was apparently painless and he had been preparing for it for so long.

My sisters, Carol and Susie, and I determined to fly out as soon as possible from the East Coast to Carmel, California, where our father and step-mother had lived for many years. In the confusion of our travel arrangements we found ourselves booked on separate flights, which afforded me hours of solitude to absorb this new internal landscape. I was keenly aware of my own sorrow and of the frailty of Angelika, my father's wife of almost forty years who was now confined to her bed. How would Angelika receive this loss?

I was six when my parents were divorced, and my sisters and I grew up feeling that there was never enough of our father to go around. Carol, Susie and I visited him on some weekends, and we shared vacations together, but his life as a market researcher in New York City felt somehow distant and exotic. I did not welcome the news of his remarriage when I was sixteen, and meeting Angelika did not improve my reaction. I felt no affinity for this sharp-spoken German bombshell with an impressive job at the United Nations. Although my sisters and I made considerable effort to improve our relationships with Angelika over the decades, stories of bruised feelings were legion. In the twenty years since they had moved to California, each of us nurtured special time with our father over the telephone and occasional trips to the West Coast.

In recent years these cherished phone conversations included forays into various arrangements for long-term care, hospitalization and death. I was concerned that the distance between us would make it difficult to be supportive of my father and Angelika in their time of greatest need.

Now, on this flight to California as I held unprocessed grief over the sudden loss of my dad, I faced the most challenging scenario I could imagine — a grief-stricken, bedridden Angelika surviving my father and needing care and supervision.

What follows is my account of the journey that began that day.

2: I JUST GOT HERE

With a six-hour flight from Boston to California on my own and so much to process, I take up my journal and write, hoping for clarity to emerge. I have found that sometimes when I write my feelings, then wait in silence, I am rewarded by messages of love and wisdom which I record as they emerge, with the understanding that they come from a wiser spiritual place.

Journal: November 6, 2006

"Hello, my dad: you died yesterday morning, or sometime in the night. I miss you already. I feel the loss of you in this realm ... that we won't share conversation about meditation and spiritual truths, that you will not listen with such loving attention to all the details of my life ... that I will not see you and hear your voice. But I think of the fatigue I've heard in your voice since Angelika's recent hospitalizations, and I understand. Your body has held out for so long ... you must have been so tired.

"Perhaps you can show me now (or when you are ready, for I guess now is a time of transition) how to continue this spiritual conversation. I know that it is possible. And Carol, Susie and I will be connecting with Angelika. We won't forget her."

Resting in my airplane seat, I begin to drift off and unexpectedly have a sense of "presence" behind my closed eyes, a sort of circular glow of light. Waiting with anticipation, I begin to inwardly hear the familiar cadence of my father's voice speaking into my mind. Baffled and excited — not wanting this to be interrupted, but anxious to record the message — I reach for my pen and journal and receive....

It is so beautiful – you cannot imagine ... full of glorious, joyful beings. Light, weightless, no pain (I hadn't realized how much pain there was in my body.) Very free.

Struggling with disbelief, I'm looking for some affirmation that this is real, some concrete proof. But the next clear sense is the feeling that my father is struggling with concern for Angelika and needing to know that she will be all right. I try to reassure him that somehow she will be — that he needs to trust this process. Then I sense that he is having trouble conveying the gladness of it....

I write: "Do you see your dad?"

I know that he is here – I haven't seen him yet. But there are other beings ... Yogananda ... beautiful, light beings full of love and tenderness.... I have the sense of being surrounded by wisdom. The air is full of deep knowledge and there is beautiful sound coming from everywhere at once, as if the song of everything is heard. And "here" — where you and I share this moment — I see as if through a veil. I see how limiting and limited it is and I want to share this joy of the Completed Realm.

"Tell me something!"

You are on the right path, Jane. Angelika will really appreciate your ability to communicate with me, if she cannot. Please keep in touch with her — just keep letting her know she's not alone.

Taking in the seriousness of this request, I write: "I will."

Then — I don't know why this pops into my head, perhaps because his great love and temptation was culinary: "Do you miss food?"

Not at all. All feeling is so open. It's as if I'm tingling everywhere with pleasure – no hunger or desire for more.

"Is there something you'd like to say about this trip to California?"

Enjoy yourself. Please don't be put off by my empty body. I'm not there, Jane. If seeing it helps you to know that – go right ahead. But I'm here, and so very joyful. We've had a good time. I mean, we've really grown in each other's lives. You've taught me so much, and I hope I've given you something, too. You were very much on my mind in the past few years — and in my prayers.

What I see here is so different — so much more wonderful than I could imagine....

"Are you tired?"

It's different from that. It's blissful — I'm taking it in....

"Was it hard — when you died?"

I didn't know it! I didn't know what happened. First I went to bed, really tired — I've been so tired lately — then I wasn't there! I mean, I felt different.... It was a little confusing, but you know, I was ready, too. I was holding on there at the end. It was a relief to let go. I can't tell you what a relief it is.

Feel free to share this with your sisters — the parts you think they'd like to hear. I'm so grateful to you girls — you women — for thinking of, taking care of, Angelika. I can't tell you.

You'll learn something about reality, Jane. I mean it. It's so hard to see it from there.... I guess that's why we get a glimpse of it in dreams and things ... and with people like Yogananda and Jesus — the great beings.

Jane, it's all right if you feel uncertain here. Don't worry about it. I mean, I think it'll get clearer in time. Don't worry about whether it's "real" or not. You'll see what I mean!

"Have you seen Jesus?"

Not yet ... I just got here!

"You seem happy."

Everything I've ever wanted is here. It's like seeing 360 degrees for the first time — but that's the full spectrum of everything: Hopes, dreams, beauty and joy....

"Am I really speaking with you?"

Well, yes, Jane. I'm real. I'm as real as I've always been. I guess more real in a way.

"I feel like I should let you go — to get settled in or something...."

This is really good for me, Jane — talking to you. It eases my mind, too. Because I have nothing to worry about here, and, you know, I'm still letting go.

"How can I help?"

I guess ... receive this — and I know you will. And doing what you're doing — with Angelika and your meditation. It's really wonderful what's happening with your writing....

I'm going to miss seeing you girls.... You know, I couldn't stay.

"I understand. I'm so glad your passing was painless. I'm loving hearing from you, too! It's what I've hoped for!"

Well, we both have.

"This is a lot for me to take in!"

Well, sure it is! And, you know, you don't have to work at it.

"I guess I'm afraid it won't happen again...."

Well, I'll be here!

"Is there more you want to say to me?"

Just thank you for sharing this with Angelika. I'm really looking out for her and I really love her and I want her to know that. I'm sorry I didn't have a chance to say good-bye. And I wish I could be there for her — that's my one regret. I just have to believe she will be all right. You know, I couldn't stay. I wanted to be there for her. I really didn't mean to leave her.

I feel he is upset ... "It's all right, Dad. You need to trust that it will be all right — that Angelika will be all right."

It's hard to do.

(After a silence....)
This is not an ordinary day — this is my glory day. Thank you for listening.

You know, Jane, I've been looking forward to this for a long time — just like jumping into space and being caught up in something truly wonderful. I've been getting ready for this for a long time. I'm really excited about this. I couldn't be happier.

I only wish I could be there to care for Angelika. You know, it's hard for her to accept help from people. I just want her to know how great this is. I want her to look forward to it. And we can take the next part of the journey together.

At a layover along the way to California I telephone Angelika, who sounds exhausted. I am full of excitement about passing along my father's messages and at the same time apprehensive about how she will receive them. But remembering that she was very open and grateful for the meditation I offered during her recent health crisis, I somewhat tentatively tell her: "I heard from Dad on the plane." I hear the enthusiasm in her voice as she says, "I was wondering if you'd hear from your dad!" And so I share with her his extraordinary messages.... There is a tender silence and finally she whispers: "Thank you."

Mrs. Smith: Your Husband is Deceased

Arriving in Carmel in the evening, Carol, Susie and I approach the Smith home in its beautiful retirement community atop the mesa. The doorbell is answered by an unfamiliar caregiver whom I instantly hug — somewhat to her dismay. It occurs to me that, like us, she has just arrived here and is taking it all in. What opens before us is a small home of faded elegance full of the trophies and clutter of a lifetime: Asian vases and prints, Angelika's metaphysical books and tapes, our father's self-help books stacked beside novels and mementos of his naval years in World War II, and the walls of files and boxes of assorted storage. In our father's study there are the recent piles of CDs and DVDs that he was using to help navigate his new career: The journey to the Other Side. Black headphones occupy his leather easy-chair, where he would listen for hours to messages from New Age gurus as well as the ancient religious mystics and sages. I am impressed by the extent of his preparation. And now, as if he had been "beamed up" just before our arrival, only the empty chair remains.

My sisters and I take in a collective breath as we turn the corner to our step-mother's room. It is the breath we've always taken, steeling our emotions against her brisk Germanic dismissal. It's painful to admit the extent to which we resented Angelika. She took our father away. There was always the fear of ruffling her feathers, and the frustration that we had to earn our father's attention by keeping our step-mother satisfied.

Ahead of us are piles of boxes, tables of tissues and pills, a motley collection of stuffed animals, a walker and a large prosthetic leg. To our left, enshrouded in her hospital bed, is the shrunken figure of Angelika, looking so pale and lifeless that we reflexively lean in to check her breathing. We awkwardly arrange ourselves to face the bed: What is there to say? "We're sad. You're sad." Mechanical. It was always our father we had come for.

As if summoning all of her strength, she thanks us for coming and rehearses in disbelief the announcement of her care-giver yesterday morning: "Mrs. Smith, your husband is deceased."

I feel a breath of tenderness for her then. How can I feel angry at one so utterly helpless and alone? The awkwardness remains, but the vision of her frailty seems to suck all the bitterness out of me.

A Messenger for Harry

The next morning my sisters and I have convened in our guesthouse room to arrange our priorities. What is our game plan? Our father's body has been taken north to San Jose by the Neptune Society for cremation. My sister Susie, a long-time hospice worker acquainted with this part of the journey, wants to see our father and say goodbye. Carol, the eldest, has been trained in shamanic practices. She would like to perform a ritual ceremony to send him on his spiritual journey. After some internal struggle, I have decided to stay behind and visit with Angelika.

Journal: November 7

"Hello, my dad. I decided not to go see your body, though I'm grateful that Carol and Susie will bless you on your journey. I'm hoping to hear from you again as I wait here alone...."

I would love for you to be with Angelika today, honey. That would be a gift to me. I want to be there for her. She's a real trooper. She's fought really hard. She's my girl.

"Is there anything you'd like me to say to her today — on top of yesterday's messages?"

You know, we came out here [to Carmel] *together, she and I. And we had a good time, overall. We did well. I couldn't have wanted anything more. I didn't want to leave her like this. I'm trying to figure out why it happened.... So you could say we're both trying to figure it out, she and I. And if she figures it out I hope she'll let me know! I'm so grateful to her, for everything. She's the best companion a guy could want. We've had our struggles but, you know, that's life. I've grown a lot thanks to her.*

Now as I write his words I feel that he is addressing Angelika directly:

Oh, honey: I'm sorry to go so suddenly. I miss you so. I'm working on being with you — letting you know I'm there.

There's so much to learn…. You won't believe how wonderful this is. I wish I could describe it to you. I'll be sending you more messages. We aren't so far apart.

Well, that's it for now, I guess. My love is with you. I hope you know that. I hope you can feel it.

I'm feeling quite overwhelmed with a strange mix of joy and grief, wonder and trepidation. On top of missing my father there is this miraculous communication of his joy in the afterlife. And now there are intimate messages for his wife. How can I share these things with her when we have been so formal with each other all these years? These words are so deeply personal, beyond any conversation I have ever had with my step-mother. We seldom conduct a discussion of the weather without discomfort! How can I be the messenger for these intimate words of love?

The sense has come to me quite clearly that my father would love for me to be with Angelika as much as possible in this time. It is a tender and awesome request. I wonder if this heaviness I feel is also a by-product of being the conduit of such powerful messages. I am a stranger in a strange new land.

I wait quietly for guidance, and out of the emptiness comes the awareness of a benevolent spiritual presence and a message begins to form itself in my thoughts….

Speak these words with humility —
simply, truthfully … just as they have come to you.
Trust. We are here. Harry is well: He is with us, in Spirit.
You are a messenger for Harry.

This out of your relationship with him —
your love for each other,
your work together in the realm of spirit.

Rejoice in this. Let it be a celebration and a confirmation.
This is what you've wanted!
It is here.

Following Angelika's afternoon nap I enter her room with the old palpable awkwardness. Small talk quickly falters and I ask to sit beside her bed, struggling to make a comfortable spot amid the boxes. I know by her expectant look that she is hoping for one thing — another message from my father. As I read his words aloud from my journal, I feel her soften. She listens with great emotion: She knows her husband is speaking to her.

You're Never Alone

November 9:

I'm feeling a little bubble of joy here in guesthouse number 6 as I relax into this open morning where I can stay in bed, looking out over pines and canyons to the distant mountains while sinking into this new internal landscape. I've telephoned friends and advisors back East who are helping me to find my bearings. My sisters have returned home, and now there is time to simply *be.*

Yesterday we had a little ceremony on the beach in South Carmel. At Carol's invitation, my niece Fay, my sister Susie and I gathered shells, feathers, stones and driftwood and formed a sacred circle against the backdrop of crashing waves, wide sky and crying seabirds. We celebrated Harry Lee Smith, who loved the sea and learned to love the great eternal mysteries as well.

Later we learned that by some cosmic coincidence, our father's ashes will be scattered at sea on December 7, the anniversary of the Japanese attack on Pearl Harbor. He was there. He saw it all. The berth where his destroyer was to dock had been completely demolished. Our mother had once told us: "I decided if he survived the attack I'd marry him." He later survived a Japanese suicide bomber's dive into the smokestack of his destroyer in the Pacific: He was awarded medals for his courage and ingenuity in helping to navigate the damaged ship back to port in the Solomon Islands. No medals exist for navigating the wounds of war: Witnessing the shelling of his gunnery crew, the tensions of constant vigilance, the years at sea.

I'm waiting and hoping for a message this morning, but it is a long time coming and this causes me some unrest. At last I feel my father's presence and pick up my pen to write....

Don't worry about anything, Jane. I mean that. It's harder to speak to you now. I'm kind of further along with this thing.

It's so beautiful ... I really get caught up in it. I'm learning such wonderful things. It's pure flight, and I'm becoming part of it ... so words are harder now. But I'm sending energy to Angelika, and they assure me that she won't be alone. You know, we're still together — that's the amazing part.

To Angelika:
Angelika, honey, you'll be here soon. Don't worry about it. It'll be fine. I know that. And <u>now</u> you won't be alone either. You're never alone! That's what I was really starting to feel before I left ... it was all so peaceful. The shifting is really pretty easy. You just let go. And they take care of the rest. I mean it. It's just the way I hoped it would be ... only better.

Jane: I have assurance here that you'll really be taken care of. All you need to do is focus on this work – and what great work it is! I'll help, too.

Yogananda is here with me — I guess I told you.... He has a school here (aren't I lucky?) And it's open to the light and sky — so beautiful. We always feel his presence — and his teachers ... all opening to the Pure Divine Realm. The school is sort of built into a hillside — with many levels, like layers of terraces with one side all open. And what we see I can't even describe: Glorious. So I'm settling in here.... You can just imagine how this is: No pain, no weight of any kind – such great energy. There are lots of schools, lots of amazing places.... And you can travel just by thinking about it!

"I'm feeling like Angelika will be all right, Dad."

Well, that's a great relief. I wish she didn't have to go through this difficult time. When you get here you realize how much hard work it was sometimes.... It hasn't been easy for her.

*You know, honey, that feeling you woke up with — that's what
I'm feeling here now: Joy.*

In the afternoon I share these words with Angelika, who
visibly brightens as I read and re-read Harry's words. As
I prepare to leave for the East Coast, I try to reassure her
that our contact will continue and that I'll return as soon
as possible. We've begun a pattern that will deepen in the
coming months, of sharing together these messages while I
am in California, and speaking as often as we can by phone
when I return to my full life in New Hampshire. It is a bit
wrenching to leave her to her solitary existence. Apart from
Delora Ann, the excellent social worker who oversees her
full-time caregivers, she has few friends in her community.
It isn't for lack of effort on the part of her neighbors. Most
overtures are met with chilly distance. I don't know why:
Any questions I've asked about her early years in wartime
Germany have been met with the same cold silence. Now her
isolation is intensified: Apart from her metaphysical studies,
her husband was her life.

Think of Fire as a Completion

November 13 – New Hampshire

Just a few days after my return home, I learn from my sister Susie that this afternoon our father's body will be cremated. This is very painful for me. Alone in my room, I'm crying and asking, "Dad: Please help me to hold this." Soon I feel a familiar presence....

I am not there. I am not in that body. Your dad is here.
Your dad is well and strong.

"This is really hard for me!"

I know. I understand.

I have this impulse – not 100 percent sure it's from dad — to drink a toast to his voyage. (Can someone give Angelika a cocktail?) Then I have this thought: You have a choice — to feel your sorrow, which is real and true, or to feel his joy. Feel both! Why not? This is the riddle of life!

Tell Angelika she is not alone. I am with her — tonight, and every other night, and every day, until we see each other face to face again. She can rely on this.

"Dad: This is still so hard for me — when I think of your body consumed in fire.... Help!"

I understand. Think of fire as a completion ... as part of a ceremony of life, part of a cycle. I have thought well about this. It sits well with me. I know Angelika shares my thinking about this. I hope she is remembering our conversations. Maybe she can share them with you. Remember: I am not in that body. So this is a good solution. It's a fine solution. Think of it that way.

In the evening I call Angelika, who is delighted to hear I've received more words from my father. I read them over twice and she affirms: "Yes, your dad and I both felt this was the best way ... we talked about it. It was what we wanted."

3: RECEIVE ME

December 27:

Through the many holiday preparations I have checked in frequently with Angelika by phone but am aware of her perpetual loneliness. I know she would love to hear a message from my father. With a house full of our combined family's needs and activities it's been hard for me to find the time to meditate. At last this morning my silence has been rewarded with a poetic message for Angelika from the voice of Spirit.

The curtains will part, the way will open....
Light beings will come, surrounding you with gentle love.
Are you afraid of anything? All is gentleness and love.
Are you worried? Rest in our tender care.
We are together now.... It won't be long.

Know that we care for you in even the smallest detail.
Begin to relax in our care.
Let go of the things that tie you to this place.
Release them, like unnecessary baggage.
The journey is light and easy — we are together now.

Begin to surrender yourself to our presence all around you....
We have always been near you. Now we come closer....
We come to free you from the worries and cares of this world.

When you close your eyes you begin to see us,
dancing like golden sunlight. We are here.
Everything that you wish for is here with us:
Your deepest heart's desires will be met ...
your sweetest dreams.

Feel the whisper of Joy:
As if from another room, Joy summons you....
Strange, at first, to hear her voice, like a little bell
or the sound of a running river.
Like a faint soft breeze, Joy comes —
your little sister, dancing by your side....
She will always be with you now —
begin to welcome her and listen for her voice....

Even great sky angels come for you, preparing the way.
See how loved you are! How special!

Do not worry about anything. Rest in our arms ...
We are together now. We are one.

In the evening I telephone Angelika, grateful to have a message to share with her but hesitant about the intimate nature of it. I can feel her emotion as she takes in these words. There is a pause, and then her quiet reply: "That's beautiful. Thank you."

December 30 - Carmel

I have traveled back to California to be close to Angelika after an absence of six weeks, but am feeling somewhat stunned. The trip has taken an unexpected toll on me. My head aches and I feel far from bearing any spiritual gift at all.

It seemed so right as I hastily planned this trip the night before last. I'd had a slightly incoherent conversation with Angelika and then asked to speak with her latest daytime care-giver who said she'd had a fever and seemed disoriented in the morning: Maybe she had suffered a minor stroke. Back on the phone with Angelika I asked her about these things.

"Maybe it is happening now" — the dying, she meant.

And I said: "Maybe it is. Would you like me to come out there?"

"Yes. If it's all right. Yes."

So here I am, head splitting and feeling as spiritual as a train-wreck even though I know this grace that unites us is a rare and special gift.

Following a long morning in the guest-house I venture out into the warm sunlight to visit with Angelika. She brightens as I enter the room, and I reconnect with the excitement of our shared journey. I offer to read back over all the messages, which is moving for both of us.

After a few quiet moments, Angelika speaks of how she and my father had hoped to die together, in the same moment. I feel the immeasurable sorrow of her being without him here and wanting to make the journey to him. She says that this communication we're receiving is what she lives for now. This is true for me as well, after the decades of hurt and misunderstanding.... We are both grateful.

Lay Your Burdens Down

The next morning, alone in my room, I drink tea and take something to quiet my headache. I gaze out my window over the lush Carmel Valley. Soon a sweet comfort fills me, and I begin to seek guidance for Angelika, whose sole desire is to join Harry in the Spirit World. A warm spiritual presence gently impregnates my thoughts ... I write:

Angelika is trying hard to receive me.
She may be gentle with herself.
Think of "Self" as a creature that has traveled the long
and difficult terrain of this earthly journey.
Like a great camel, crossing many deserts,
Self gets up and goes forth each day in search of sustenance
in a land that is often dry and unforgiving....

And now, Angelika, I ask you to lay your burdens down.
The journey is finished.
You have been faithful to your mission on this earth
and I call you home to my arms.
I am the Source of life and love and sustenance.
You do not need to seek any longer the earthly sustenance.
Everything you need I will provide for you.
Rest, and receive me.

We surround you now.
Even in the corners of your room and beside your bed.
We are here to minister to your needs
and make safe your passage.
We come for you. Rest in our arms.

Knowing it is her deepest desire, I ask: "Will the journey be soon?"

"Soon" is not a meaningful measure. We are here now,
accompanying Angelika on her journey,
which has already begun.
Part of the journey is her experience of it, her surrender to it.
It unfolds as she allows and embraces it.

"Receive me," is what I ask. I am the source of all Love.
I am Love — a power so vast and infinite
none on this earth can grasp it.

I am the call of each atom to the infinite source.
Each tiny particle clings to every other particle
for Love alone. There is nothing else but Love.
"I Am" is the cry that holds the universe together
and causes the spheres to dance in space.
I Am all there is.

This uniting force which calls all of life unto itself now comes
— sending a sweetness of angels – to call Angelika to myself.
As she receives me she is making this journey.
Every time she inclines her soul unto my love,
she is moving closer into my embrace
and releasing the faithful creature of this body
which has made its long earthly journey
and fulfilled its task.

Such is my love for Angelika, such is my care for her,
that I have given her messengers —
both in body and in spirit.
Now I come to her unmasked. Soon I meet her face to face.

Angelika: Release this body and rest.
I am the source of all Love and Life and Joy.
I Am.

Feeling delighted to have such a beautiful message for Angelika, I rush to her home across the mesa. As usual, her head is propped up by a stack of pillows and she is resting and reading a couple of newspapers. I am reminded that in her job as secretary to the German Consul at the United Nations, she would read several international papers before breakfast. Today she feels a bit uncomfortable. As her body gradually slides down the bed's incline, pressure builds up in her tailbone, and this in turn increases the pain in her "phantom leg" that was amputated eleven years ago.

I've watched the care-givers move behind and pull her up by her shoulders until she rests comfortably again. This is the only position her body can tolerate. I ask if I can pull her up this time. "I'm heavy," she responds.

"Well, I'll try."

There is a time when we've made the secret passage from a place outside, observing another person's life, to right there beside them on the journey. And we are able to rearrange a worn, uncooperative body on the bed ... prop up a head, an arm, rearrange an incomplete leg. There is no distaste. It's a little magic that has happened. First there was chilly distance, now there is familiarity and tenderness. I refer to the stuffed animals by name, replacing the cap usually worn by Alphonse, the giant frog. Then I'm ready to share the morning's beautiful message from Spirit.

In the evening, I read all of the messages aloud to Angelika and Delora Ann. This tireless social worker, deeply moved, asks: "Aren't you exhausted after this?" How easy it is to underestimate the cost of spiritual work. It's all invisible, and there isn't much that one actually accomplishes in the process of waiting and tuning in to these sweet frequencies. But imagine plugging yourself into a great generator and conducting an extraordinarily powerful current. Of course I'm feeling spent.

The next morning, in the quiet of my guest room, I'm soaking up the landscape and drawing my little wagons in a circle. Resting my head, being gentle, just watching the light grace ancient pines as they slope down into the Carmel valley. I'm seeking a message for Angelika and for me, as I'm still feeling a bit weary and looking for strength.

Do not be concerned for Angelika in this moment.
Angels are assisting her on her passage.
There will be other messages
and they are a great grace and blessing to her.
She needs to release to God-self which is all around her now.
This is her passage and she is in every moment connected
with the presences in her room.
She needs only to "tune in" to them.
This reality will be more and more central to her awareness
as the other preoccupations slip away.

Tell her simply to cease to be concerned
about the timing of this passage.
It is inevitable.
She is releasing in one reality —
the appearance of this world —
even as she is deeply awakening to the continuous reality
of God's omnipresence.
Soon that will be the source of her existence —
her air, her food, her provision.

When she is ready, the great release will occur.
But to her it will seem only a sweet and continuous journey
into the embrace of the Beloved.
Perhaps she needs to be reminded that she has
more power in this process than she realizes.
This is her passage, and she is co-creator in the journey.
And that in itself is a grace.
Deep within herself she has chosen
this timing of following Harry.
It is not a punishment but a grace.
Harry is a face and an embodiment of God's love,
and now she has the possibility

to experience God's love directly.
What does this mean? It is a deep mystery.
Angelika may ponder this mystery even as she asks
Divine Source to speak to her, touch and hold,
love and guide her. She has requested this passage.
She is at the center of this deep dance of love.

At last to understand that she has never been alone …
God's love has always been calling her home.
The stage is set for her.
The helpers are present.
We wait upon her acceptance of our love.

A Conscious Transition

January 3, 2007

In this morning's quiet I've been rereading my early communications with Dad just after his death. I ask if he has a message for Angelika now. After a few moments, I feel the warmth of his presence....

Angelika, honey, I'm here for you. I know it's hard to believe sometimes. I love you so much. I'm sorry this time is difficult for you, but I know that beautiful things are happening at the same time. Imagine that I am in this room and I am helping you ... helping you release everything else and come with me. I'm lifting you and you don't feel the weight of anything anymore.... You're light ... you're floating on air.

Imagine my arms lifting you and taking away all the pain and all the difficulty. Let your head be light — your heart, your arms and legs ... you are weightless. It isn't difficult at all. You just let go. Every time you imagine this — every time you feel outside of your body, or tune in and feel the love of Spirit all around you — you are moving out of your body.

It won't be long. You're on your way. I want you to try to be aware of all the helpers who are there for you. (I should say "here for you," because I am here, too. There is no distance in the Spirit.)

In a sense you could say you're here now. We are together now. Your mind can practice taking that in, and one day there'll be nothing in your mind saying it isn't so. I think maybe that's how it will be. Because it's your mind which is really telling you we are separate. It seems a little crazy — but I promise you you'll understand this soon. It'll all make sense. And you'll be radiant with so much joy.
You'll really understand what Joy is.

So just practice little by little shifting into this consciousness: That what is Real are the spirits all around you – the "unseen." And of course it isn't all up to you. There's plenty of help from this side. You'll need to do very little.

You're making a conscious transition. I see that now. So that's pretty special. We are both learning something together on this one. And maybe this is something you'll be able to teach others along the way. We keep learning. We'll be learning a lot of things together. I'm learning something just by watching you. And Jane is learning something, too.

Your inner treasure is shining. You're my girl.
I love you.

Happy Birthday.

So many times I doubt these messages: Am I making them up? How much of my mind is interfering with or editing them? But these words have come like a song, and I've simply recorded. I had forgotten that it was Angelika's birthday!

I cannot describe the emotion this message stirs in Angelika when we read it together in her room. Her eyes fill with tears and she looks down at her hands....

"Would you like to hear it again?" I ask.

"Please."

January 4

I have time for a last visit this morning with Angelika before leaving for the airport. After speaking about plans for my return in a few weeks, I reread my father's birthday message and suggest we sit in silence. After a while, I feel his presence in the room on the other side of Angelika's bed.

In shared silence, we are soon enveloped in a sense of loving bliss — a gathering of Light. I speak its message of gratitude and blessing for this experience shared by the three of us: Dad, Angelika, and me.

On the way to the San Jose airport, just over the hills north of Gilroy, I pass into a valley crowned with the most substantial rainbow I have ever seen. I pull my rental car to the side of the road to phone Angelika, and by the time I reach her there is a double rainbow stretching the full width of the valley.

"Do you think it's a sign?" she asks.

Sure do.

4: WHAT IS "SOON"?

January 25 - Carmel

After weeks of barren New Hampshire winter it is blissful to feel the warm sun on my first full day back in California. I sit outside savoring the brilliantly colored landscape, grateful for the respite from some hectic weeks at home and looking forward to two weeks of a schedule focusing on rest and meditation. The birds are alive with myriad fantastic songs....

Spirit whispers:
We are here.
Thank you for coming.
The day is full of blessings.

I notice birds circling overhead and have the sense that Harry is here in patient protectiveness.... Listening, I begin to feel his voice:

Angelika, do you feel my presence? I am here with you, always beside you, until we are in the same energy form — then you will understand so much and see so much that is unclear to you now. You know that I love you, that all is Love. All is permeated with the essence of God-self, which we call Love.

You could say that the doorway you are entering is Love, and Love is the way. So whenever you feel something that is joyful or pleasurable or that brings you peace, just breathe that in, and exhale what is not peace. It's a simple exercise. Notice the goodness — people's good intentions, a gentle touch, a kind word — breathe it in ... and exhale what is not good and gentle and kind.

And when you are alone, notice that I am with you. I will keep bringing you little signs of my presence. Breathe these in, along with the love I bring, along with the love of the unseen care-givers and angels who are here with you.... Breathe in their subtle energies, and breathe out the sense that you are alone, that you are handling all of this alone.

When I stand outside of my true self, I do not understand either the timing of this, and why it is I cannot be there in person to help you. But that part of me, I know, is not real. It is not the part that is infused with enlightened love. For there are mysteries here — in this space of expanded consciousness — just as there are mysteries there. Here we breathe in, or expand to clear consciousness. We are one with divine intention.

And so I hold this mystery in perfect peace. I love you perfectly as I am here beside you, and I wait with you in a state of sweet acceptance. Divine intention — over-will, you might call it, or the river of Love's wisdom — flows with a brilliance we cannot comprehend. We simply can inhale the wonder of this mystery, and exhale all worry, doubt and fear. For it is known that you will be as I am soon. And as we sit together, let us practice acceptance, peace and joy. We, together, breathing in what we cannot yet understand, and releasing our resistance to it ... accepting the gifts it brings: For I am assured that they are many.

Keeper of the Flame

This afternoon for the first time as Angelika and I meditate together in her room, I am able to voice aloud the messages from Harry and other spiritual presences. Although it feels strange at first to voice another's thoughts as they enter mine, I begin to relax as Dad articulates his love and gratitude that we are here together, learning so much in this period of Angelika's conscious passage.

Angelika asks: "What is 'soon'?" And: "Is there something else I still need to do — taxes, bills?" A long silence follows. I have the sense that Harry doesn't have the answers ... that we are waiting on Spirit. At last we sense a presence of singular force, and speaking with the voice of a wise old shaman, I address Angelika:

You are offering yourself as a place for this great mystery.
Like a fire, it is warming our hands and giving light —
healing, cleansing light.
Many beings are learning from this mystery.
Like a fire at night, we gather round it,
and we thank you for offering yourself for this.
The fire will not burn forever.
You are the keeper of the flame:
When the fire goes out, you are no longer in this body.
Your task is this offering: To be faithful to this mystery.
It has nothing whatever to do with the bills.

We sit in silence together following this surprising experience. Although it is a somewhat ambiguous answer, Angelika is satisfied and quips: "Anyway, that's what you get when you ask a shaman."

In the evening I walk the beach and wait for the nightly show: Sunset in Carmel. How like the fire of Angelika's passing....

Many of us gather on the shore to see the intensity of this final glow, and if you stare at it, it seems to last forever. But close your eyes and it is gone so fast it takes your breath away.

January 27

I want to speak with Angelika about money. Yesterday she voiced the concern that one of the reasons she wishes to die quickly is to preserve some inheritance for my sisters and myself. This needs to be discussed: Of course it would be great to receive an inheritance, but would I trade it in for more time with her now? Absolutely. My desire to help her make the journey of this death soon has been in response to her profound sadness and yearning to be with my father. So clearly we need to talk about this.

Sitting by Angelika's bed in the afternoon, I hesitantly broach the subject of money. It's an awkward topic in any case, but between us there was never much genuine warmth. And yet I find myself cherishing this time together; if there were no spiritual messages from the other side of death this would *still* be a miracle in itself. I need to say it, and she needs to receive it. We have a new relationship now.

She listens as I make it clear that the money doesn't matter. All of the inheritance may be used up and we will still figure out how to meet expenses and take care of Angelika, even if it means bringing her across the country. The old boundaries between us are gone. Even as we're both wary of this slightly painful discussion, I feel a barrier lifting. She looks directly into my eyes to thank me.

Then we settle into our new pattern. I sit beside her bed and after asking for protection and guidance we wait together in silence. After ten minutes or so I feel my father's warmth, and he begins a wonderful message through my voice which I later record....

Angelika: I am here with you always. You are releasing now, releasing your ties to this material reality.... This room is a bit like a "de-densifying factory," where material weight and lighter spirit are separating. We three share a space where thin veils shimmer between worlds. Though even now I seem to be in another space, I am in fact here. There is no "there" or "here" – all is here, now. We are not separated by my body's death. There is nothing to worry about, nothing to fear. So little that I worried about in that life was of any real importance.

I see you even now light and flying, your face radiant with joy.

Neither of us is anxious to close this beautiful meditation, and I try to hold onto the perception that it is all here now — all that lightness, freedom and joy.

Who Lifts Me Up?

Today Angelika wants us to search for another answer: "So, when the fire goes out, I die. There is no more work I need to do. I am faithful to the fire.... So this is what I need to know: How do we do this? Who will lift me up? I cannot do it by myself!" This very practical concern comes from one who has lost half of one leg and has used a wheelchair for over a decade, one who can no longer sit up unassisted.

We begin with long silence, and after some time I sense a spiritual presence:

We are Many and we are gathered here for Angelika,
to assist her in her passage.
We come as messengers of Glory and Light,
spiritual midwives who delight in their mission.

Imagine a walnut breaking open to reveal its core:
Angelika will experience a momentary physical crisis,
and when the attention is diverted,
we will come and lift her spirit for its glorious release.
We delight in our task, especially when the body
has become a restriction to the soul.
And Harry will be right by Angelika's side. He will be there.

The midwives are here now. The journey has begun.
We do not know the time of it.
It is as if Angelika is on the platform and we are here
to take her bags and lift her onto the conveyance.
Her only task now is to release. If she begins to worry
— about taxes, for instance — just hand it over to us!
Release your baggage....
Like migrating birds in formation;
When the leader flies to the rear,
another takes its place,
but the leader must fall back....

Imagine a river of continuous spiritual life
and release what is not pertinent to this reality.
All the things within this household
— relevant to the material world —
are less relevant to Angelika
as she becomes aligned with Source.
As she allows and receives their wavelengths,
the helpers send their golden threads
to hold her in the journey....
And she create a space of silence within —
Not focusing on will or intention or concern,
but simply receiving.

These midwives are very good at their job —
they have done it many, many times —
and they delight in this work.
They are here and their frequency is strong.

It's thrilling for us to receive such a beautiful and specific answer to Angelika's question. A bit like Mary at the Angelic Annunciation we "ponder these mysteries...."

5: FORGIVENESS

January 30 – Carmel

My daughter Susan has phoned from Massachusetts with the stunning news that her father is being airlifted to Brigham and Women's Hospital in Boston. Apparently he had been feeling ill for a few days, but there was no warning for his sudden collapse this evening. His symptoms suggest a ruptured aneurism in his brain. I struggle to assimilate the enormity of this news.

Doug Bernhardt and I have been divorced for almost a decade after eighteen years of marriage. He has remarried and lives nearby in Massachusetts with his wife and two young daughters. His relationship with two of our children is severely strained. Our eldest daughter Jessica — the child of my first marriage whom Doug adopted when she was quite small — has been out of touch with Doug for many years, with wounded feelings on both sides. John, the youngest of our three grown children, also suffers great frustration with his father's emotional distance and apparent lack of interest in his life. Susan, our middle daughter, has the fullest relationship with her father and his new family.

As I sit with this alarming news, I struggle with conflicting emotions — shock, concern, and anger that Doug might leave this life without addressing a legacy of disappointment and pain. My first reaction is to cry out: "You can't leave now — you have work to do!" Overwhelmed, I ask for spiritual guidance. In the silence a message begins to form and I take out my pen and write....

Doug is not going to die right now.
He has to find the courage to stay.
He has work to do,
and if he quits it'll only be harder next time.

With humility he needs to reconnect with earth —
he has a job to do, with his children, family, friends....
He fears he can't be forgiven, but he can.
We roll up our sleeves now and go on.

He <u>can</u> hear now. Say, "We forgive you — now fight and grow."
He came here to grow, but has been dominated by fear.
This is his opportunity for freedom and release,
and to do good with his life.

He has to stay here and heal. This wound is a healing wound:
It gives him a pathway.
It is a severe mercy.

How Do We Receive?

Having made hasty preparations for an overnight flight to Boston, I enter Angelika's room with sadness. We sit together with the enormity of the East Coast developments and our disappointment that I will leave tonight. She is gracious in acknowledging my priorities — certainly I need to be with my children now — but I can feel Angelika's heaviness. Our time together has been a balm to her weary spirit.

We have time before I need to leave for the airport, so I ask if she has a question for today's meditation. Tentatively she voices her most pressing concern: "How do we receive God's love?" Over and over the direction has been to receive, but Angelika quietly confesses her difficulty in this. After gentle urging she admits to feeling unworthy of love.

After a long silence in which my mind struggles with anxiety over Doug's condition, a message begins to form in my mind and I find words to speak it aloud:

Unworthiness is like a doorway. If Angelika says,
"I want to receive you, but I feel I don't deserve your love,"
this is a doorway for the Beloved to enter.
This tender admission has opened her heart,
providing a pathway for release,
healing, and acceptance ... for mercy and grace.
This increases the light everywhere, and also strengthens
the bond of Angelika with Source (Love ... Light),
which is her passage.

"Is there more I need to do?" she asks again.

No. No. No.
Just receive me, receive the lover of your soul
who longs to hold you and see you face to face....

Angelika asks: "Is Harry the lover?"

The Lover is the source of all, the creator of all.
Harry and Angelika have been students together.
Harry will always be here.
He is loving this process with you, and learning so much.

I feel my father's presence, and he addresses the new development of Doug's stroke and my premature departure as being difficult for both Angelika and me. But he assures Angelika that he is here:

In some way we can't understand, the timing is perfect. Trust this. Now the work is in accepting and entering more deeply into this dialogue with the Lover. The process has begun — all the helpers are here. How beautiful it is to participate in this opening to the Beloved and in this dialogue. God's radiance is sent forth into all the universe — and there is no creation unworthy.

The feeling of tenderness for Angelika is so strong that I am moved to hold and stroke her arm — how loved she is!

The I.C.U.

February 3 - Boston

Seeing my ex-husband lying in a coma in the Neuro-Surgical ICU is almost more than I can bear. As I struggle to read aloud several of the Psalms he loved, the unbidden memories come in heavy waves: Our early years when Doug juggled seminary studies with tutoring to support our young family; the thrill of his ordination to the Episcopalian priesthood; the churches where our children sang in choir and Doug delivered sermons; Easter Sunday services with all the preparations and the joy of Resurrection ... fragrant hyacinths and lilies passed out to happy parishioners as they left the sanctuary.... Where are these living fragments in this sterile room where a man's body lies bloated and inert within a mechanized maze of life-support?

In my bed at night I search for God with an aching heart: "Help me.... Please speak to me!"

We are here. You are faithful: Know this.
Doug's journey is his own, his own mystery.
Just as Angelika holds the mystery
of her life's great passages,
so Doug is at the center of his own great mystery.

"How do I pray for him?"

Hold truth. Be still.
Center yourself in your own deep origins.
Know what you know. Do not be afraid. Trust in me.
This may be a great healing opportunity. You do not know.
You are not charged with knowing.
Be faithful to your own journey.
Where are you — where is Source for you?

"O.K. Tell me."

We are here ... just as we were "here" in California.
We bathe you in light and love. Breathe, drink, receive.
This is all you can do in this moment.
Receive us. We are here.

Later in the day I phone my spiritual teacher, Greta Bro, who is helping me to accept and honor this challenging journey. In my fatigue I am easily overwhelmed by these miraculous openings, which are somehow a gift and burden at the same time. I don't know how to hold all of this! "Rejoice," Greta says. "This is Doug's opportunity. The soul finally gets its way."

"You are learning to see with spiritual eyes. Death can be a doorway of transformation. All is well. Wait and return to Source for guidance. Your channeling is profound. Imagine that a book is closing on your old life with its doubt and insecurity, and another book is opening. This requires radical trust." Good words from one who is further along on this journey.

I Think it's About Forgiveness

I have been praying and meditating for Doug but have felt very little ability to connect with his spirit. My sense has been to trust that his journey is his own, with its own wisdom, timing, and mystery.

But tonight, while briefly rushing through the grocery store for soup and soda for my son John, I received a clear communication from Doug. Another person might doubt the synchronicity of this — but I am sure it was a direct message. Doug, the long-time drummer, adored Don Henley — drummer/singer/song-writer — and often sang his songs, with a voice that closely resembled his. As I stood in the soup aisle, I was suddenly aware of the speaker directly over my head broadcasting Don Henley's voice singing to his ex-wife: "And I think it's about forgiveness / even if, even if, you don't love me anymore...."

At once I felt a rush of all the hopes and dreams, sorrows and pain.... The urgent river of forgiveness with its merciful cleansing left me sobbing. Doug could not have conveyed his message more precisely. Reaching home I find my journal, take up my pen and ask: "Doug, what else?"

I don't know where I am, but I'm here.
Something's happened.
I miss everybody.
Who'll take care of the girls and Ari? [Doug's wife]
Susan's been great. God, I love her.
Jessica came to me [in the hospital]. *God, she was amazing.*
I don't deserve this.
I owe John so much. Wish I could give him something.
I've failed him and you. I wanted to tell you that.

"Doug: You can go on and do what you have to do. Leave some grace for everybody. If you did it for me (in the market...) you can do it for them."

I will.

"Trust your guides. Do the best you can right now. All is forgivable. Now go on: Do what you need to do. Move on, as you need to.... There'll be more healing opportunities."

In the evening I share news of these communications over the phone with Angelika, and she responds: "Be prepared for more messages from Doug."

Hope

February 8 - New Hampshire

I awaken to the strange sense of inwardly hearing Doug's thoughts. Mechanically, I reach for a piece of paper and write:

So I'm feeling a lot of things. And I'm feeling hopeful for the first time in a long time. I'm still not sure where I am but there's some kind of sense of freedom, and I feel God sort of the way I used to, and sort of a new way that's more concrete. I feel as if everything happens for good, and I haven't felt that way in so long.

I'd been feeling so discouraged and worried about everything. And I know it was me. I felt trapped. I'm really sorry to everyone who may have felt like it was their fault. I had freedom and I didn't use it. I don't know how better to say it than that I couldn't use it. I don't know why. I'll probably find out why. The sense I have now — that's really new — is that there isn't any judgment. As a concept, it doesn't exist.

I'm thinking about all the people who came to see me and all the things they must have felt. Even though I was far away then — I don't know where I was, but I was very confused — I could hear what they were saying. I just couldn't understand why they were saying it.

There was so much love. God, what will Emma and Charlotte [his youngest daughters] *think? I can feel bogged down again when I start to worry.*

I have a feeling I've left that place and that life and I don't really know what's next, but a lot of heavy stuff is gone. And it isn't a bad thing. It's as if I'm here — wherever that is — and I feel somewhat more hopeful and lighter. And I feel like everything that happens is somehow good.

You should have heard the things people said to me! I feel so grateful — though I didn't register then. I don't feel pain. The body there isn't where I am now.

6: MESSAGES FOR OUR CHILDREN

Doug's remarkable outpouring continues and I keep writing. Now he is addressing his words to our middle daughter....

Susan: You've been so great. You've always been more than I deserved. You've been one of the brightest lights in my life and I guess I want to say there's no point letting your light go out over this. I think you were trying to shine for both of us — to make up for what was shut down in me. So stop it, OK? Because I'm here, and there's more light and I'll learn what I need to learn. I'm feeling pretty determined to learn. I could say I'm sorry till you get tired of hearing it: I'm sorry for not seeing and supporting you better, for not deserving all your love, for leaving so soon.... But the thing I'm really holding on to now is forgiveness — that's my big liberating word.

And we have to forgive. It's really powerful. You forgive me. You forgive yourself. I forgive myself. And then you shine. Let your light shine. Don't let anybody take that away from you, Susan.

You're my special, special girl. Don't let anything get you down. Try to learn from this. That would be the best thing. Life doesn't end — that's really clear to me now. We keep getting another chance.

You'll feel me.
You'll know I'm here.
You'll see me again.

Let yourself feel all your feelings — sadness, loss — but then please, please move into your life. That's the best gift you could give. I'm not gone — I'm very much here ... in a better way. I don't know much right now, but I know that. And it feels good to have my head and my thoughts beginning to clear up again.

Give yourself every chance — don't ever give up or feel trapped. There are apparently Light helpers everywhere. I'm getting it now.

I love you so much.
No goodbye.
I'm just getting clearer as I go. Honestly.

The transmission from Doug continues with a message to our son and I keep writing....

John: I've failed you so much. I tried, but I kept getting in my own way. It was what I thought — that I was trapped ... that I couldn't do it. I made that trap for myself.

I failed you. The only thing that softens that now is these helpers — I think I'm in some place of moving out of my body and into freedom, so I feel like helpers are with me who are showing me a lot. And it's lighter and there's good feeling for the first time in a while.

Oh God, John. When I think of all the chances you've given me to be a good dad it hurts more than I can bear. But they're here. And they're showing me lots of goodness everywhere. Amazing light and possibility.

I guess what I'm seeing is we make our own traps. I have to forgive myself for being an idiot and then let it go and go on. There are so many possibilities to grow and expand. This journey isn't an end or a closing down. Everything is opening up to me ... like a great wide field of promise.

Oh, John. I hope you can get some of this. If you get it now, think how the possibilities will open up in your life. You can be and have anything you can imagine. You can do good for people. You can really love them and have a good life — then you'll look back with pride and joy.

I need to ask you to forgive me — if you can. Please, please have a good life. I'll be here — I'm not leaving, really. This part I don't get yet. All I know is that in those days in the hospital I was less "here" than I am now. Thank God my head is clearer now — that was really confusing.

Forgiveness. You ... me. Myself.
I love you, John. I always have. I always will.
We'll meet again.
The sky's the limit, remember.
Live a good life.

Do good and feel good and remember me every time, how proud I am of you. Forgiveness is everywhere. So it's all O.K. ... every single thing.

I'm on my way....

Even as I well up with the emotion of his powerful expression, I feel Doug's message continuing. Now he is speaking to Jessica, from whom he has been estranged for many years. I write:

Jessica: You were incredible to me. I heard it all but I didn't understand what was happening to me. I'm so sorry I let you go. I was so stuck. And you were just incredible to say all those things you did [in the hospital]. *I think that's part of what moved me through that weird time. I was far away and really confused. Now I'm getting clearer. And lighter. I feel like I'm getting a chance again — another chance. I get to do better, be better.*

You are such an amazing person and it's been stupidity and loss for me to miss knowing you. Can you forgive me?

The hardest part is forgiving myself. But I'm feeling — even though I still can't see much — I'm feeling like forgiveness and hope are all around us. And freedom: To do, be, create. I know I've screwed a lot of things up. I need to believe this power that I feel around me — probably divine love like I haven't really understood it — that it can do anything. Miracles — lots of them, all the time. Nothing's set in stone. Everything is moving, healing. So it's good.

Keep living your good life and I will keep growing. I'm happy to be free and sorry it's been so hard on you there. Forgive me. Forgive yourself. Seize this great life. Maybe that's my biggest mistake. Seize it — it's all there for you, all the time. Enjoy it! Love it!

I'll see you before too long. I haven't left. I'm just in another form, I guess. Anyway, I'm still here but I'm not here. I think I'm leaving the whole body-material world. It hurts that there are messes and unfinished business, but these "helpers" have been really kind to me, is all I can say — giving me some hope that everything can be healed and hope is everywhere.

I do love you, Jessica. I always have.
Thank you for giving me the gift of receiving and knowing it.

In the ensuing days and weeks, I am reluctant to share these messages with my children: What will they think and feel? But Doug's intention seems clear to me and one by one I privately offer their "letters" to John, Susan and Jessica. As he reads the words addressed to him, John grows silent: He recognizes his father's voice. Susan is moved and also concerned: Does this mean her father is saying a final good-bye?

When I share his message with Jessica, she recognizes not only Doug's voice but also the particular experience he is describing during the period of his coma. Here is her account of that time:

"I had been estranged from my step-father for many years when I got the call from my mother in the middle of the night to say that he had had a severe stroke and had been taken by helicopter to a hospital in Boston ... that the doctors were trying to save him, that he was fighting for his life.

It is strange to hear news like this about someone that you have known so well, and for so long, but haven't spoken to in years. I had been so angry with him for the way that he had treated me growing up, that many years ago I had stopped calling him Dad, and starting calling him my step-father.

Now I felt like I was transported to a time when he was in my life every day. I suddenly cared deeply about his safety. I felt alone as I lay in bed imagining him being lifted through the cold night sky. I wanted the surgeons to do their best, I wanted him to be O.K.

At the hospital, in the ICU, there was a lot of chaos, tears and anxiety. Doug's wife, whom I had met once very briefly, was there with my sister, my mother was on her way, and Doug's siblings were gathering from other states. We all converged in the hospital waiting area. I was the only person there who was estranged from him. I imagined that even though he was unconscious to us, inside of himself he was confused and fighting to stay alive. I knew he needed to hear from someone that he was going to be all right.

I felt a certain calling as a bit of an outsider in the group: I felt that my voice would be clearer to him because it wouldn't be clouded with as much of my own emotion.

I sat next to him when I could and I spoke close to his ear. 'It's me Jessica, I'm here, I forgive you. I know you are confused, but everything is O.K. out here....'"

7: IF THE FRUIT IS GOOD ...

Somewhat incredulous following this amazing outpouring from Doug, who is still alive but in a coma, I ask: "Spirit, how can I believe and bear these messages, which are so hard to hold?"

You've made yourself available for this work.
You've let me convey the importance of it,
in an aggressively materialistic empire.
Make no mistake: The empire is pervasive.
Each psyche encounters it within.
You have made yourself available to receive —
in spite of internal and external obstacles — the quiet.
You have opened yourself to stillness.

Perhaps you didn't expect so much answer
to your simple supplications.
You waited, and received a little here, a little there.
Then in came bigger presences.
But do you see that it has been a clear invitation
on your part to be of service?
That you have sacrificed, or simplified,
and made yourself available for this?
It's been your choice. And now we are here together.

"What shall I do today?"

Celebrate. Healing will occur. Rejoice: All is made new.
All is redeemed. All is forgiven.
Hope. Rejoice.

Mystery

February 9

Once again I awaken with a sense of Doug's thoughts in my mind, but I retreat from them. This feels like too much to bear.... Please help me, loving Spirit!

Rest in our care. Great mystery surrounds
the comings and goings from this earth,
and there is powerful unseen grace.

"That's good, because what we see right now is unbearable."

This is a supreme test for you:
To believe the messages of Spirit
in the face of such apparent loss and darkness.
Can you hold what you have received?
Doug's earthly journey is not fully finished.
Often it is this way. This phenomenon is not uncommon.
Sometimes a soul passes in a stage or stages
separate from the cessation of bodily life.
Each soul is held in infinite mercy as it returns to Source.
Doug is wrapped in love and mercy.
He is engaged in a positive discourse,
as you have experienced in yesterday's messages.

"All right, I will receive, if he or his helpers wish to speak."

Doug:
This is what I'm feeling! Mercy. Healing. Hope that's infinite.
I've messed up so many things but that isn't what's important.
What's important is that we keep growing, on and on, because
there's no ending to the soul's possibilities. There is no ending
to my life. I can't quite believe it yet, but it's true.

They can't wake me because I'm not really in the body now. I was terrified at first but there have been helpers who are so good to me — men I've known before who are here — with extraordinary wisdom.

"All is forgiven." I can't believe it. Do you know how good that feels? I don't have to feel hopeless about my life, even now.

"Help: God! I need help with this. It's crazy-making to receive these words from one who is still alive, on whose survival so many are depending. What am I to believe? Dad? Help!"

My father's voice enters my thoughts and I write:
Jane: There are so many mysteries here. I think part of your journey is in learning to trust what you're receiving. Look how great this gift has been for Angelika! Not a word that hasn't given her hope. You're allowing her to open her heart to God's love and healing, and together we help her passage. What on earth could be more right or perfect or important?

"Close the book on the old!" Let go of the self-doubt, perfectionism, under-cutting yourself. Your strength, sanity and survival right now are very, very important. I can't tell you how much you have meant to Angelika and me.

"How do I know I'm not making all this up??"

Well, honey, if the fruit is good, who cares? If the result is forgiveness, hope, and a more positive future, what difference would it make?

"It *is* good, isn't it, all of this...."

Of course. Why do you need to be believed? Why not leave self-doubt at the door? You're living in a materialistic world: Should it surprise you that Spirit is doubted and derided? Why buy into that? Live proudly the light that you are given. Trust it isn't madness. (Or if it is madness — I'll take some of that!) Do you see what I'm saying? This is the medicine the world needs! You've stumbled onto the medicine cabinet. Try not to be so afraid of showing it and offering it. It's what everybody really wants: Everybody wants this balm. And you've found a secret doorway. So stop doubting. Let it come. Trust yourself. Trust these gifts. What have you got to lose?

8: WE ARE HERE

You've Got A Valentine

February 14

I have spent some time addressing the needs of home —
supporting my worried children, catching up with my partner
Paul and his three children, returning to the regular routines of
a household. At last a sense of normalcy has returned and I am
able to enjoy the quiet of my meditation room. I am hoping for
some words of comfort to share with Angelika. After quieting
my thoughts, I feel my father's presence and he begins to speak
into my mind's receptive silence:

My darling Angelika,
Look at the love you have allowed and nurtured from your bed.
How loved you are and how you cultivate the love in others.
I'm so proud of you, Sweetie. I warm myself here beside you
— in the fire of this mystery. See how our attention turns from
"how soon?" to a kind of gratitude for some of the blessings of
this time. It isn't easy, but see how you are making the best of
it! How you are enabling and allowing good to come.

I am loving being right here with you, by your side. There's
no place I'd rather be. We are making this journey together:
I am always with you. You are learning so much — learning
the ways of the great Lover, the creator of all of this amazing
energy we inhabit. We are experiencing this together. I am
constantly amazed by this, that we can be experiencing this
growth and wonder together.

I love you so much.
Happy Valentine's Day, my sweet!

It feels wonderful to call Angelika tonight with this message. When she picks up the phone I announce: "You've got a Valentine!" I read it over twice.... She is so grateful.

During our regular phone calls I ask about her day and reread the messages from Harry and Spirit. In the evening she and Delora Ann study spiritual books, trying to grasp these great mysteries. On her own, Angelika rests or reads the newspaper, or rereads the messages I've typed up for her. Her position seldom changes, whether she is sleeping or awake, and she bears the tedious wait with extraordinary dignity. What a fine example: The way she holds her head....

This is a School

There is also much to be grateful for: The rich beauty of this home in New Hampshire, my loving partner and our combined family who are all healthy and relatively well.... But the demands of our household can seem relentless as I juggle the weight of Angelika's frailty and Doug's condition. He hovers in a drug-induced coma and the effects of his stroke are still unknown. I grieve for my children and myself ... for a young family's dreams and losses. I am also struggling with a lingering chest infection.

My God ... please speak.

Your hope is love. Your fear is losing love.
It is impossible to lose love.
Love cannot be lost.

We are here. Our love is here.
These are deep, quiet days. Hold close to your center.
Hold us close. Imagine angelic embrace....
Slow down. And slow down again.
Keep finding answers to the voices
that deride this pace and focus.
Such challenge can be healing on all sides.

"I often feel I'm not 'pulling my weight' in this large household as I sit quietly with my writing and meditation...."

Dad voices his opinion:
Remember, Jane: This is a school. It will never be perfect.
So if it feels messy or compromised or confusing, that's O.K.
Welcome to earth! Don't try to make it perfect. Please know
you're doing a really good job. This means so much to me I
just can't tell you. There just isn't any "right" way to do this

life. But if there is, you're doing it. I hope you can feel me here with you....

"I am thinking of going out to California as early as next week. What do you think?"

That would be good.

"I am afraid: Afraid of loss, afraid of making a mistake...."

Remember: "Love cannot be lost."

9: IT IS POSSIBLE TO LEAVE AND RETURN

February 23

Doug is awake! He is still on a breathing machine and tube feedings, but his eyes have opened and he is responsive. The damage to his brain has been extensive, and we are apprehensive about how he will recover and what abilities he will have....

Doug has asked to see Jessica and John. What follows is John's description of his visit with his father:

"I entered his hospital room and sat to his left, his weak side. The nurse who was attending to him asked me if I would like to speak to him. Since he had to be intubated he had a small talk box not unlike what smokers are forced to use after years of abuse with nicotine. The nurse kindly stated that this was just the second time he had used it and to be patient. For the first time in a long time I felt fear. Not fear of my father, but fear of what he would say, what he would remember ... me?

The nurse quietly left the room. It started simply enough.

'Hi, Dad.'

'Hi.'

'How are you feeling?'

His response to this was succinct: 'Drained,' he said.

As we continued to talk it turned into one of the deepest and most profound conversations of my life. Though simple, it was what was unspoken that impacted both of us: The feeling of warmth and love that is so simple yet so easily forgotten.

For many years my relationship with my father was strained, bent and nearly broken. Promises made and broken, stubborn fights fueled on both sides with passion and fervor. We had so much in common, yet at times we were so distant and guarded. This was simply the way of things.

As I sat with my father I noticed something that touched my soul. There was an innocence and unguarded candor that I had never known. It was as if he had been reborn to this world with the look and demeanor of a small child ready for life! He was so open and happy. Considering what he had just been through this to me was a miracle by itself.

As the conversation progressed, I began to ask about his experience.

'Dad, what do you remember last?'

'Light,' he said.

Light, I thought. So many afterlife encounters surround that basic premise of light. As we were talking about this more in depth, my cynicism began to fade in terms of my narrow past view of spirituality and all things holy.

Yes, there is life after death. Yes, it is beautiful. But why did he come back? For what reason or purpose was he here? Us. He had unfinished business.

He then said two words that meant the universe to me.

'I'm Sorry,' He said. 'I'm sorry I haven't been there for you. You deserve better.'

I couldn't speak. For so long I had longed to hear those simple words, yet I underestimated the immediate and long-lasting impact it would have on me. In that brief instant all the pent up anger, frustration and ill-will I had passionately held for so many years drifted away like a feather in a light summer breeze. I began to cry.

'It's OK, Dad. Everything is fine now.' We are here.

I held his hand and looked into his wide child-like eyes. We smiled. As far as his memory had gone, he was still Doug. He was still the man I grew up idolizing. My love for him had not gone, as I thought for so many years. It had found new life. Although naturally it was hard for me to see him in that state, I could not have been happier to have him back with me."

Within the first few weeks of his "awakening," Jessica also shares time with Doug. Here is her account of their first visit:

"When I went to see him, I was by myself, and when I came in his head was turned. As I approached him he turned to me, and there was a light and a peace in his eyes that I had never seen before.

'Hi Honey,' He said in warm and welcoming tone, 'Have you eaten?' I noticed his voice was higher than it had been, and as I talked to him more about my life, my husband and my work, I noticed that all of the barriers that I had bumped up against in all my years of knowing him were gone. He was humble. He was able to listen. He cared.

He was interested in things, he wanted me to come by whenever I wanted to, he was open and warm. It seemed like our ability to connect and enjoy each other's company and share thoughts and ideas was limitless. He told me I had the biggest heart of anyone he knew. I felt that for the first time in our relationship he could see me: that day he kept telling me how precious I was.

I really loved this person, this person who was new to me but had the body and memories of Doug. This was a Doug I loved and who loved me. It was a second chance.

I feel so blessed to have experienced this time with him, to have had a second chance with an important person in my life. To have gotten to love and connect so deeply.

When my mother shared with me the messages she had received from him while he was in the coma, they made complete sense with the person I had seen. It was clear to me that an incredible transformation had taken place."

10: SHE MUST OPEN THE DOOR

March 2 - Carmel

I am beginning a two-week stay at the Smith house in California, looking forward to quieter, focused time with Angelika at the house. Already my spirits feel more centered and hopeful. Dad's room has been cleared for me, so I will no longer stay at the community guesthouse. I have set up little altars, opened the blinds, rearranged a few things. It is quite inviting.

Little by little everything in that room begins to feel sacred to me — the dressers, the lamps, the bedside table.... The tree outside the window becomes my companion in this fearful and exciting new journey. In the room across the hall a woman I've held at arm's length for forty years is waiting to die, moment by long moment. And I have become a lifeline to that unknown place beyond the veil. Who am I to carry out this task?

Each morning I awaken to the dubious cast of all my failings: My selfishness, my irritability, laziness.... And I look to the tree and the little altar in the corner. I ask for the guidance of spiritual helpers, trying to let go of all the mental clutter and be the vessel for whatever love or wisdom might offer itself for the fragile woman across the hall.

It takes some time for me to accept the rhythm of these days: Long hours alone in the morning, a brief visit with Angelika, a drive into town to see the shops and take a picnic to the beach.... Then in the afternoon I return to Angelika's room. I've learned that promptness is important: Angelika expects me at the precise time we have agreed to meet.

I try not to show how nervous I feel with this strange role of intimacy and trust. It is clear that Angelika believes that each word I speak in our meditations is sacred guidance. Am I "right"? Am I making it up? This fearful and exhilarating tension never leaves me.

This morning, awakening to unaccustomed sunlight, color and birdsong, I ask for the Beloved to speak.

We are here.

"Do you have something to say to me?"

We do. We are grateful for your preparations.
The simplicity to slow your systems
to be still, rest, receive ... heal.
You have harbored so much in this time.
Let this be a space of haven and rejuvenation.
Try to release agenda, self-criticism and self-doubt.
You have prepared for this work,
which is our work — our collaboration. Thank you.

I am grateful to be back at Angelika's bedside this afternoon as we offer ourselves to receive guidance and wisdom for this mysterious passage of her spirit from this visible world.... Preceding our time of silent seeking, Angelika asks her most pressing question: "This is four months now, and he said 'soon.' I'm still harping on that one: What is soon? Four months is quite a time."

Following an extended period of silence, I sense a river of light – the radiance of eternal Love. To the question: "How soon?" the answer seems to come that this is like a dance....

Harry embodied the energy of the lover,
and now the dance is between Angelika and the Great Lover.
When He comes to the door and knocks,
she must open the door: Receive, soften ... allow.
This is part of the conscious passage she has chosen,
the contract made by her soul for this life:
To be one with the Beloved.

There is no right or wrong way to do this.
If there is an answer,
it is within the most intimate recesses of her heart —
none but she and the Lover of her soul have the answer.
And time does not matter:
All the bliss of divine union is here now....
There is no "here" or "there," no "then" or "now."
Spirit calls to itself, Lover to Beloved, and this is the song
of the cosmos, the vibration of all things....

Angelika: The light in you grows stronger every day
as you identify less with physical reality
and more with eternal spiritual reality....
The veil softens as you release mental activity
and learn to dwell within the space of heart.
This heart is the one who cries out: "Come" to the Lover.
And the Lover answers, "I come."

I beseech Spirit for release for Angelika from pain, both physical and emotional ... from a sense of separation.

There is no separation in this community of love.
The company of saints is everywhere....

Harry speaks:
Angelika, honey, I am here. I wish you could see all the light helpers who are here also. I wish I could describe the beauty of this realm which is both present and — in many ways — still unseen. I'm not worried about when you will make this transition because I know it'll happen, and you'll see me just as clearly as I'm seeing you now. You're going to love this so much....

The suggestion comes for us to meditate, breathing in love and — on the exhalation — sending this love into the body.... It is a rather blissful experience, as we feel the presence of Harry and other unseen companions joining in the exercise.

March 5

Today is so beautiful. I take a long walk on Point Lobos and sit for a time on a little beach watching the harbor seals as they watch me. Then I take myself out for a lunch of fresh halibut and drive on to Monterrey for shopping and cotton candy and the slap-stick show of sea lions in the bay. Angelika and I have no time for meditation as I spend hours tracking down one of her prescriptions and her nurse arrives late....

Later in the evening we enjoy reading from the wonderful *Testimony of Light*, with Sr. Francis Banks' detailed descriptions of the after-life mirroring and expanding on my father's account. Then we take up Angelika and Delora Ann's study of Dr. Michael Newton's *Journey of Souls* with great excitement, as over and over his case studies of regressions to the "life-between-lives" reveal details that are strikingly similar to Dad's descriptions of his journey — the sights, sounds and sensations at times almost identical. With each surprisingly familiar passage Angelika and I look at each other with wonder, as if we are piecing together an amazing puzzle.... For me these accounts also serve to verify the channeling process which I so often doubt.

March 7

In today's meditation with Angelika, Dad speaks of his enjoyment of this time of growing understanding and his enthusiasm about spiritual developments. He begins with a description of the release of the body:

Imagine your body as a balloon only thinly encircling divine eternal energy. One morning this balloon will pop and what will be surprising is how much "the same" you will feel, the same and yet free and joyful within the ecstatic realm.

He describes his excitement over this house he's creating (I picture a stack of glass boxes, the topmost ones looking over beautiful scenes and also actually out into space.) He's working with Yogananda, who isn't always present, and meets with small groups of colleagues in beautiful settings.... The work is hard to describe — probably because it's so advanced I haven't the capacity to grasp it. It involves shaping and combining energies in a way that is new and exciting. Dad feels truly honored to be in such an advanced school.

But I ache for the pain and difficulty of your remaining here, Angelika. I am consoled by conversations with colleagues who reassure me of the importance of this time: "It will benefit Jane, and through her many others." But as important and precious as this time is, Angelika, you may decide to leave if it's too much, and there will be no judgment, none at all.

As difficult as it is to describe, you have perfect freedom here. You can participate in spiritual work and communication even now, as you receive infusions of divine Light and begin to assume the limitlessness that will soon be your total experience.

I also had hoped we would make this journey together and have struggled with pain over this, but please remember that I am with you continually. Even as I am creating the house and studying in the school I am always here and when summoned my attention is fully present.

Do you feel the veil between us getting thinner?

Donkey Jane

March 9

This morning I awaken to inner darkness. I'm so aware of my limitations and the ways that I keep falling short of my own expectations: I overeat, stay up too late, don't exercise enough.... On any given day I can find scores of ways to hound myself. It is hard for me to make good choices. I don't know why. Maybe it is the heaviness of this earth itself: To inhabit a body is a heavy thing. Am I being a perfectionist again? What does one do when one wakes up heavy and dark? Spirit ... help!

We are here. We understand. This life is not easy. You are on your true path and this is what you need to remember. You look to your strong beacon again and again, and this is what it means to be faithful. This is not an easy journey to navigate. Remember that perfection is impossible within this energy substance.

Accept your humanity. Love tenderly this human animal. Maybe, like St. Francis, you can name her ... Donkey Jane. And sometimes Donkey Jane feels just like a mule: "I won't get up; I won't go out; I won't do work.... Go away and leave me alone."

You can say: "OK, Donkey Jane, you've been a good companion to me. Now go rest. We'll be all right. I'll wait for you." Spirit can talk to body!

Look at how she has served your visions: Traipsing to Auschwitz and Hiroshima with all the challenges.... Touring and performing and toting heavy props and exhibits.... She does all these things you ask of her. And now you are channeling powerful spiritual energies while traveling back and forth to California with a chest infection. So she wants to watch a movie and eat sweets and stay up too late.... Do

you see? Maybe you push her too hard sometimes. Be really
merciful with this body, Jane. Give the donkey a rest!

In today's afternoon meditation with Angelika, *"I Am"*
addresses us with a gift of energy infusion and healing....

I Am ... I Am ... I Am....
Alpha and Omega, beginning and end ...
the root, the tree, the branches ...
the waves of sea and matter and energy ...
the all of all ... there is nothing which is not myself.

You, Angelika, are mine.
I am the mystery. I am the fire.
(All separation is illusion.)
I call you to myself, Lover and Beloved.
You are myself. I call you home to me.

We thank body, which has done its faithful work,
and we release the fire of self.
This is not something you can understand —
this seeming separation, this change of changelessness....
For I am all in all and I am mystery.
I call you to myself. I Am.

March 10
   For today's quiet time with Angelika I decide to write the
message as it comes instead of speaking it aloud, to preserve
and record the language of the original.

   After a silence, I feel my father's presence and write:
Jane: I am here and I want to speak to Angelika, and I want
to tell her how much I love her. She understood and accepted
me in a way no one else ever did, and I was and am so grateful
for that.

We could have such good times together. Remember, honey, how much fun we had? It's funny, but having this space when we're partially separate has given me lots of time to reflect and feel grateful ... because I am so grateful for our time together.

I think you're doing the best you can with this time, and so am I. Sort of "hanging out" and seeing what happens.... The whole thing is new and kind of surprising when you think about it. I get to practice shifting in and out of this space, and you get to practice pretty much the same thing, from your end. So one of these days we'll meet in the middle, and what a joyful reunion that'll be!

I want to tell you something I haven't said: You were always beautiful to me. I can still picture you at the time we met and on through the years.... But you have never been more beautiful to me than you are now. I mean that with all my heart. Your inner beauty shines like a jewel. And the outside's pretty good, too!

Remember: I'm always here, right with you, right beside you.

Her eyes brimming with emotion following my reading, Angelika whispers: "That was beautiful!"

"Would you like to hear it again?" I ask.

"Please!"

11: TIE UP THE CORDS

March 11 - Carmel

There is a special flavor to our time together this afternoon. We begin by sitting together in silence.... The message I seem to be receiving in meditation is:

Tie up the cords. Tie up the cords in the human life.
Speak of what is and has been.
Speak the truth of this human journey.
Embrace its sadness: Say what needs to be said.
What happens in this world is also of consequence.
Speak of the distance you have traveled together.
Do not be afraid to speak the truth —
this binds the reality of the journey.
It's not all about disembodied spirit.

In your conversation you make sacred the embodiment.
For it is not simply a container, this body.
It is a blessed vessel and should be honored and thanked.
Perhaps Angelika can speak of her gratitude
for her earthly journey.
Perhaps this is a form of closure
— a way of saying: "Thank you."

Before sharing my own message, I turn to Angelika and ask: "What came to you?"

She answers: "I was just thinking about what we have been doing here, which is wonderful. It is a great gift that we are getting here, from Spirit, and from your dad.... And I don't know how long I'll still have to wait but at least we're doing something worthwhile."

I ask: "If you could thank your journey, what would you thank?"

After a moment, she answers: "That I met your dad and that we had almost forty wonderful years together." We share silence in the great emotion of these words. "I think that's about it."

In the next morning' solitary time, I feel a subtle shift and ask: "What is coming, Spirit, can you tell me?"

We are here. Feel your own inner guidance.
It was never your job to intervene for Angelika indefinitely.
You have been faithful to the call....
Now a deeper, quieter dance takes over,
between Source, Angelika and Harry.

Jane: Your only job is to be faithful in your journey.
You are not often given a glimpse far down the road.
A faithful messenger does not open the message
or read the letter...
she bears and delivers it. This you have done.
Release now ... gracefully, simply.

I ask for clarification: "Would you please speak to us together in meditation, in a way that we both understand?"

We will.

In afternoon meditation with Angelika I record these words:

Angelika: We are the voice of the flame.
We speak now directly into your heart.
You have strengthened the ears of your spirit
and you have learned to retreat
from the immediacy of this present material form.

Now — in these days — we call upon you directly
to listen with your heart
and withdraw your mind from the throne of your being.
When you wake and when you sleep, cry out
to the great Source: "Come!" Receive, and receive again....

There are unseen messengers to whom you now align
your mind, your soul, your heart....
And these unseen messengers prepare your journey
and your way. Do not worry about anything:
The way is secure, the path is prepared,
your place is here, with us. Your Beloved awaits you.
All will be revealed to you in time.

All that you need to know now is in your grasp.
You have everything you need.
Rest in the fullness of my arms....
Rest in the mystery of time....
Rest in the ending which is a great beginning....
Your powerlessness is power: Trust this.
My strength is made perfect in your weakness.
Cleave to my strength now as the source
and sustenance of your life.
Cling to me now as both ending and beginning:
Offer yourself continually into my care.

The alignment now is True.
Let me weave you back into my loving embrace,
thread by thread....
Yield yourself to this beauty:
Yield your incomplete understanding
to my complete and perfect care.

Be assured that there is nothing now
which is unknown or undone.
Timing — in your earthly understanding — is of no importance.

It does not exist. You are even now in perfect freedom,
living your life in the completed realm.
Yield therefore to what you do not understand
and trust the great I Am,
the source of all, who loves you and calls you to himself.

There is relief from all the burdens of this life ...
cleansing, sweet water to bathe the weary traveler.
There is rest, and there is peace,
and there is gentle release from all cares....
There is lightness here which the earthly body cannot know ...
ease and flight for the earth-bound soul.

Come to this place of rest: You are welcome.
Your arrival is eagerly awaited.
When you come there will be joy as even now there is joy.

Your being grows lighter as you release your earthly bonds.
Yield to this subtle process....
For we surround you as helpers and friends.
We are here, preparing the way.

*   Dad speaks:*
Angelika, I'm here, as always....
As Jane prepares to go, remember I'm always with you.
Just try to let it all go, as the helpers are saying.
Yield to lightness, and healing,
and to the love that surrounds you....
Imagine my love, multiplied countless times,
in unimaginable ways,
filling this air around and within you....

Let that life go now, like a dream ...
and soon you will remember this eternal space,
which you have never really left.
This, here, now — your true home.

I am here with you, honey.
Just keep remembering that.

After moments of silence, I ask Angelika her thoughts about this lengthy message.

"That's beautiful: I would like to have a copy."

Mist Rising Skyward

March 16

Finding time together in the midst of my preparation to return to the East Coast, Angelika and I receive this parting message:

We are here. We fill the air of this room with our presence....
Many beings are here to accompany Angelika on her passage.

"Do you have a message for us today?"

Do not be anxious about anything.
All the words spoken here are true.
Take them into yourself as if, instead of oxygen,
you were breathing heaven itself when you inhale.
Take this love-breath deep into your being
and enjoy the pleasant sensation it brings,
for there is nothing difficult or burdensome here.

Rejoice in this: The departure is close.
Allow, rest, receive us: We are here.

On the plane trip home, sinking into my fatigue, I open my journal as the message begun earlier in the day seems to resume....

We are here.... We are always here.
We are grateful for your openness,
and for allowing your humanity to become more porous....
All is well. The shell of illusion softens
and allows truth to penetrate,
and so you see, feel, taste that all is one:
We are one heart, one self.

We are one flesh, one blood,
one continuous vibratory impulse....

The rain and the dew and the small still pool
are sisters to the ocean,
brothers to the running stream.
The sun embraces hearth-fire with benevolent kindness:
She has many children.

And so it is with human flesh —
dark and hard, soft and light....
The infant and the soldier and the beggar who is blind
close their eyes, and dream the ballerina.
Who of us does not know this human dance?

Angelika returns:
The going and the coming are mysteries to the human mind
whose muscle persists in definition, separation.
All is one place.

Death itself is mist rising skyward
... no less water, no less air ...
no less the love song of everything to itself.

Angelika dreams the culmination of this destiny —
and in the dreaming too the mist is rising....
She allows the porous flesh to remember its energetic home
before it called itself 'body,' and carried, for a time,
this flame, which is the child of Light.

And even now, here, as you grieve you feel her process —
separated by words like Space and Time....
The release is accomplished.
Simply put: There is nothing more to do or try.
"Rest" is the only directive...

Love is the companion. We are here.
We rest, we love, we trust the great Lover.
We embrace the fire.

Learn to speak without words and think without forms.
Follow thought in its downward course to the sea ...
to the stillness ... to the great opening of Light.

12: THE OTHER SIDE

March 28 - New Hampshire

I need to record last week's extraordinary visit with Doug, who was transferred to Spaulding Rehab Hospital after awakening from his four-week coma. Our daughter Susan had asked me to accompany her there, and I prepared to go with a mixture of dread and anticipation. For many years there has been painful distance between Doug and me, fueled on my end by resentment that he has alienated two of our children. I have shouldered the parenting alone. I wondered: Who will I meet at the hospital, and what is my relationship to this person? How damaged is he, and will he remember a spiritual encounter during his coma…? Already he has expressed love and forgiveness to John and Jessica, but how will he greet my visit …?

It was astonishing to see him, as he was reclining and yet awake and alert and somehow quite different from the Doug I had known for thirty years. There was a puppet-like rigidity to his form, his eyes bulging from his face and focused as if each particle of perception and each second of existence were intensely important. Susan greeted him with a hug and sat on his bed and I sat in a chair beside him, unsure of what to say. I decided there was no point in making small talk: This reawakened Doug did not seem the sort who would appreciate that.

I looked directly at him and said: "You've had quite an experience." If possible his eyes got bigger then. For a long moment he focused intensely on me and whispered at last: "You have no idea!"

I continued: "You decided to come back…." He turned to Susan and said: "Do you know what we're talking about?" She shook her head. "The Other Side," he said with elaborate precision. Yes, he had chosen to return, he continued. He had seen his mother, who said nothing but knew everything. It was difficult for him to receive her because he was trying too hard. "I was always doing that."

By now I knew that the transmissions I'd recorded during his coma had been real, however miraculous, so I reminded him of the infinite forgiveness and possibility he'd experienced. "A blank check," he echoed. I reminded him that when things got difficult he should remember this: That he could have stayed there, but he chose to return.

He shared with us the vision he'd had of all of our children playing together in perfect peace and joy "with nothing hanging over their heads." Part of the reason he'd returned was to heal the wounds. Embracing Susan, he told her how deeply he loved her and how grateful he was that she had never lost confidence in his recovery. Tears moved down her cheeks as she returned his love. Then he turned to me and said: "I love you."

Moved and unsure of what to answer, I said: "I'm sorry ..." sorry for the misunderstandings and the pain.

With the same focused intensity he said: "So am I. It's OK. We're human."

I mentioned the people from our past who had visited him in his coma, whom I remembered from our long years in Christ Episcopal Church, where we were married and he had last practiced as a priest. "The last time I took communion was from you there," I recalled.

He became very quiet then and began to focus all his attention on one repetitive motion with his right hand. It obviously required great effort for him to slowly move this wrist back and forth as if sowing seeds, his gaze intensely serious. After watching this for some moments, Susan asked: "Dad, what are you doing?"

After a pause, he answered deliberately: "I'm giving your mother the Eucharist."

My heart has been stretched by the intensity of this encounter. I am awed and grateful but also weary from the immense power of this time. Here is a man who has journeyed through near-death and transformation, a man whose brain has sustained extreme damage and who now faces extraordinary obstacles to physical recovery. And here is a child-like heart washed clean by waves of glory.

The years of our estrangement have been erased. His love for us all is so intense I shrink from the fire of it. Even as I feel it would be generous to visit him again, something in me knows it is too perilous a journey. It is almost as though the unfiltered love awakened in Doug's heart is too brilliant for this place. I begin to recognize that I have been given a treasure, and it is enough. I rejoice for our children, that they are witnessing this miracle of love and forgiveness.

13: INFUSIONS OF LIGHT

Back home in the ensuing days, I seek the quiet of my little meditation room. Aware that I haven't received a message for Angelika in some time, I ask for guidance: Her bed-bound days are tedious and long....

Be still. Stillness is all there is, in the center of all that is.
Angelika will make the ascent.
Tell her the waiting is a sanctified waiting.
The stillness has purpose. The emptiness has meaning.
The wait is an important process in her unfolding journey.
Let her contemplate the fullness of this emptiness:
The charge of angelic messengers above and beside her ...
the training of her soul to allow, receive ...
the knowledge that her husband is beside her,
in invisible form ...
the knowledge that her experience will enlighten and comfort
the lives of others....

The strength she develops in this waiting
is essential to her journey, essential to her preparation....
Make no mistake:
Great spiritual presences surround her.

Harry speaks:
Angelika, honey: I know that you are weary. Believe me, if I could move this thing along for you, I would. I'm trying to understand it right along with you, because it's baffling for me, too. But I wish you could see the light everywhere here. I wish you could feel the energy of love that's here. I mean, it's real and it's everywhere.

I guess what I'm asking you is to feel it with me. Join me sometimes just in breathing in and receiving this light and love that is all around us here. It's not make-believe — you can experience it, just like when you eat or drink.

Maybe part of the mystery of this timing is that in this conscious passage you've chosen you wanted to really experience everything, and part of that is experiencing what is already here now. So you can think of this as a training period ... for feeling and receiving, and noticing the fullness in what seems empty.

Start by feeling me here. It's like developing a new sense organ: Tune everything else out for a minute and let yourself feel something new ... an awareness deep inside that you are not alone, even when the room seems empty. For starters, I'm here. So start with me. Just feel me. I know you can do this. O.K.? Try.

April 15

Several days pass before I again speak with Angelika over the phone. I worry about her isolation with a sense that I should be there to ease her pain, but as I ask and listen, I begin to hear that she is sinking into this solitude: "I rest a lot and I've given up being interested in much that is happening. I'm talking to your dad a lot more than before." Apparently she speaks to him, then often has a "thought" in response: Like the thought that there are still a few things to do, so she'll be here a bit longer ... and Dad doesn't know how long.

When I respond, "See, you do have intuition," she compares her perceptions to mine: "I don't channel the way you do."

"But Dad didn't ask you to hear all his messages, remember? His only desire has been that you would know he's here. You wouldn't speak to him if you didn't believe he was listening, would you?" It is a lovely moment, this mutual realization that

Harry's request has been fulfilled: She knows he's here ... she speaks with him. She rests with increasing peace.

By this time I have recorded so many important messages that I've begun to think they should be shared in publication. Angelika likes the idea that her journey might benefit others.

I read to her the latest meditation I've received:

We are here. We are full of great compassion for Angelika,
who is much loved in the Spirit realm.
The Beloved is always with her.
Harry is always with her.

She is receiving deep grace in this time.
She is receiving divine communication
at new levels within her spirit
as she breathes these light emanations
deep within her being.
She is transformed in this time
from a mortal being to an immortal one.

Angelika: Do not underestimate the progress
of your journey in this time.
You are learning to feed on Spirit, to listen and receive,
to rest and allow.
You are becoming a channel of spiritual voice and light.
Your mind is releasing and your heart is accepting....
And so perhaps you feel more emotion. This is good.
Allow this feeling to expand the receptor sites
within your heart.
As sorrow comes, let it cry out from the depths of your heart:
Help me! Come to me! Release me!
Whatever your heart longs to say.... The Beloved hears.
The Lover is already with you,
but this increased communication strengthens
the very pathways of light that will enable your ascent.

Understand this: Your ascent occurs in any case,
without any effort on your part.
But this fruitful period enables a more conscious
and glorious passage.
It is a truly, deeply blessed process. Look, within your reading,
your meditation and your conversations,
for confirmation of the rightness of this process.
You will find it mirrored back to you:
The truth that greater light awakens in you now,
and this is a blessing. Your passage is a blessed one.
The rays of light will spread far and wide.
It is a beautiful offering, as if you were performing a service,
not only for your own soul,
but for many who wait in seeming solitude and darkness.

We thank you for allowing this process ...
for receiving these infusions of light and god-consciousness
within your earthly plane. We honor you, Angelika.

"Thank you, Spirit ... beings of light.... What may I call you?"

Call us messengers of the great I Am.
And understand that we are not lofty ones.
We, too, are simple servants. We wait on the Beloved....
We delight to serve.

"Dad...? Do you have words today?"

Jane: Thank you for all that you are doing. I know it isn't easy,
believe me. I struggled so hard in that life, always trying, like
you, to better myself. I understand. It is hard to find peace.
But you are on the right path.... You are hosting Spirit, if you
know what I mean. What could be better than that?

What pleases me is that Angelika and I are in communication
now. I can't help thinking that if she can talk to me and begin

to listen to me, it won't be long before she is released. But the time doesn't really matter. We are together now, and I am so glad she knows that.

There is silence on the line when I have finished reading these words. At last Angelika says: "Maybe you could include that in the book."

April 27
In today's meditation I receive a lovely exercize for Angelika....

Angelika: We wish to speak with you about
the infusions of light.

As you rest and as you receive gentle light vibrations,
allow yourself to imagine these energies
spreading throughout your body.
You do not need to believe with your mind,
simply imagine light energy filling
the whole space of your body.
Picture a mirror beneath you and imagine all that light
moving right through every part of your body
and being reflected in the mirror.
If there is any part of you that feels dense or dark,
imagine the light energy contains magnetic particles
which attract and transform what is dense or dark.
Allow this energetic process to move throughout your body.
This gentle transformation can continue,
hour by hour and day by day....
And as you allow this process please remember:
This alone is real.
Everything else is a passing show.
The dance of light is abiding and eternal:
It is the source of all life.

You, Angelika, are shifting form now....
You are consciously choosing to leave
the heavy world of matter and body
and re-enter the abiding realm of pure light.
Nothing of your essence is lost in this transition.
All that has enlivened your body
is contained within this invisible light energy.
Indeed, your mind cannot conceive of the nature
and source of this light,
because your mind itself is a passing manifestation.

Simply relax and breathe light ... feel light ...
begin to identify with light.
Lie upon the mirror and see the light
radiate throughout your body....

You may begin to think to yourself:
*I **am** Light ...*
*I **am** God.*

After reading this message to Angelika and telling her about how our little book is shaping up, I ask if there is anything she'd like to say about herself to include in the manuscript. I don't know what I am expecting — she is such a private person — but it feels important to give her the opportunity to voice a few autobiographical thoughts for the book. After a pause she very carefully articulates:

"I don't know how soon I can join my husband in the Spirit World. I will always be grateful for those forty years of mutual love we enjoyed on earth."

14: INCREASING MINOR COMPLICATIONS

May 8 - New Hampshire

When I phoned today I learned that Angelika has become anxious about the possibility of needing to go to the hospital for a minor procedure. I'm hoping through meditation to find some reassurance for her.

"Spirit ... what do you have for Angelika today?"

The time is nearing when she will have
increasing small complications,
and she may welcome these, as signs of the progression
of her journey, her exit from this world.
All details of procedures will be carefully nurtured
within the great grasp of the invisible helpers who support
her in every way — physically, emotionally, and spiritually.
As she embarks on this process,
she may take this excellent opportunity
to reach out her hand to the Beloved.
He alone will miraculously release physical concern.
Any such process is like a dress-rehearsal for the moment
when the Beloved's influence will be all in all.

If there were any sort of concern here, we would inform you.
For you are not a child, but a woman who needs
to fully participate in each phase of this journey.

Thus it progresses. And, strangely, it will bring you joy.
For you will know that these progressions
are the predicted preparation,
and that the glorious release will follow ...
as springtime follows the arduous winter.
Do not waste your precious time in worrying.

Harry will be with you, as always,
as will all the helpers and guides you need.
You are much loved, and we do not neglect our own.
Your path is a radiant one,
of which moments of your journey on earth
have been but a pale glimpse.
Your glory will shine like the sun.

Love is here, in its unchanging, abiding form.
What is of decaying substance
now betrays its mortal limitation.

And how beautiful this is!
Behind the mask of matter
we perceive the ever-abiding face of God.
And so we breathe and sleep and move in love alone.
This is a precious moment, Angelika.
You and the Beloved are one.

So rest, relax, receive.
All is well, and all will be well.

I've made arrangements to fly out to California next week to be with Angelika, and she seems to relax as we discuss our upcoming visit.

May 10

The pain within me these days is palpable, yet mysterious. I am beginning to suspect this pertains to Angelika. Please, Spirit, speak to me. What is the source of my soul's heaviness?

The curtain between worlds seems, from this side,
to be a heavy, dark barrier.
It seems to close with a definitive weight ...
and this is the source of your sadness.
It is the source of all mortal sadness: The weight of death.

And it is the doorway to immortal illumination:
The gift of death.

Are you afraid of Angelika's decline ...
that a gift so recently opened will be lost?
You dreamt the event — do you remember?
Some months ago you dreamt of her passage,
as if you were in her body ...
how she stood and how she walked
(for the first time in over a decade)
and how she greeted Harry.... You felt the amazing joy.
This is what you must hold for Angelika now.
This is all that is real ... all that will be real.
She is dying soon, and this is the passageway to Light.
She will have wings of light and she will leave
this body's mortal cage with great joy ...
and there will be rejoicing in heaven
as two lovers are reunited.
Do not grieve over this.
Remember: The end is the beginning ...
it is the doorway to eternity.

This feels hard to bear right now, as the tender connection between us has grown so strong in these months.

Angelic Harmonies

May 21 - Carmel

Last night I arrived here exhausted. Giving Angelika a bound version of *Words From the Spirit World* (the tentative title of our book) was very moving. I sat beside her bed for over an hour as she read it through.... It was emotional for both of us. I realized: I can't imagine what she's feeling now, as I could see that she was crying several times.

"Thank you," she said. "Thank you. I didn't realize there was so much! This is really beautiful...." I responded that we're both passengers on this trip.

We welcome our afternoon meditation, and in our shared silence, I begin to receive....

We are here.
We are here in different levels of magnetic resonance.
There are different layers of angelic presence:
Hierarchies of angels....
If you had attentive ears within your energetic particles,
you would hear beautiful music,
as our many frequencies create melodies and harmonies
of ecstatic beauty, the multi-layered chorus of divinity.
This music has purpose beyond
the sensual pleasure it brings:
Its purpose is creation itself — configuration, alignment....

Sound vibration is a great instrument.
Like an intergalactic "imaging device,"
our music orders all of creation.
Angelic presence in the form of musical vibration
Is in fact what created this world and all that is within it.

Dad speaks:
Angelika: I am loving spending time with you. We're working together, even though you don't see me. I'm in the dark about

this process, as you know, but I'm always with you. It seems like they've turned up the volume on this music. What I mean is, if you were at a distance, you'd see that there is a concentration of angelic or energetic activity here in ascending chords ... really quite beautiful. (I know it's confusing to describe sight and sound at the same time, but they are the same.) There's light here, and very beautiful angelic music with many parts, many voices.... I don't think my passing was anything like this!

For just a moment, let yourself imagine that we are at a concert together....

One thing I do know: All of this will be crystal clear to us in time. We'll understand that it is just perfect, just the way it is ... down to the smallest detail. Love makes no mistakes.

Angelika listens with great emotion and says: "I was just speaking to your dad while we were meditating and he has been helping me a lot." Just today the visiting nurse had difficulty with her intravenous PICC line, and when he said: "If I bring you to the hospital they have a treatment to unclog this..." Angelika thought of Harry and it became unstuck!

Behold the Beauty

May 22

My fatigue continues. I've slept all night and half the day. There is persistent pain in my chest and my cough is worse. When I came by Angelika's room in the early afternoon and said maybe I should stay away for fear of giving her my cough, she quipped: "That would be a bit boring!" And I agree.

In spite of Angelika's powerful response to last night's message I feel dispirited and discouraged.... "Spirit, will you speak to me?"

Deep sorrow is passing through your body.
The journey between worlds is profound.
Do you suppose being a partner in this passage
is an easy task?
Do not look for confirmation of this work
in places that have no comprehension of it —
that is, most places.
Your society is so immature as regards
the passage between worlds. Simplistic. Ignorant.
That in itself is a great source of sadness.
Do you suppose there would be so much greed
and cruelty and senseless slaughter
if the people of this world could grasp in their hearts
the tender beauty that surrounds each mortal life?
Oh, yes: There is sadness in the holding of it.

And so you must let it go.
Release the work that is not your work.
Many helpers are present to assume these tasks
of bearing and birthing.
You are tired now.

Now listen, listen well: Cleave to the Beloved.
This is your strength and your sustenance.
It is not your calling to suffer any more!
Shake the dust from your feet! Do you understand?

Only turn your attention to the call of the Beloved.
If there is a task for you,
you will be given the grace and bounty to perform it.
Do not seek what is not asked of you,
nor be confused by the clamor of a million squawking voices.
Silence is your surest guide.

You may create a space for solitude
and seek refuge often there.
Go as you feel inspired to go.
Let bliss be your guide, and love your food.
Within this space you may behold
the true beauty of this realm,
and this beholding will be the highest gift you can offer
within the dense din of planetary travail.

Behold the beauty. Cherish the joy. Rehearse the reverie.
Let your spirit dance as if there were
no misguided mortal illusion —
for in truth, there is none.
Each soul will cherish her true home one day,
as sight and sanity return.
Help birth the beauty by beholding it!
Let this be your pleasant task.

And rest, my dear.
The day of burdens is past. Lay them down forever.
You are here now: We are one.

Following this rich meditation, I'm able to join Angelika, and we sit together in silence, seeking....

After a few moments I recognize the nudge of unseen presence and pick up pen and paper to write. Harry speaks:

Angelika: I want to lead you into this world of wonder. I want to walk with you into this place where you will feel no pain, no weight, no sorrow or loneliness or fear. I want to introduce you to this great family of spirit helpers and show you the glories I have prepared for you. I am so excited for you to come. I don't know when I've been this excited. Having you here will multiply my joy.

You've been so good: You've been really strong. I don't know if I could have hung on the way you have ... so patiently. It seems to me you must be able to see us soon — we are so close. And it is all so gentle and good. I know you've been fearful about certain things. It won't be a problem. There are no problems from here on out. Anything you think may be an obstacle will just be taken care of — I have assurance of that. Picture it going well. Picture me holding and guiding you ... and picture joy and relief and a whole new life....

Words fail me. I can't communicate all of this. Dream the best dream you can, and it is like that. Better. Dream of everything you want, everything you hope for, and it is yours. These pictures and dreams will help you to perceive the frequencies that are here, lighting the way. Hold out everything that is positive.... Anything else — you can be sure — is an illusion. It is all perfect and good. And soon! It's soon. This much I know. Soon as in now, I guess, because it is all here now, as we have been reminded.

Keep doing what you're doing: Talking to me, resting, allowing.... I'm smiling and loving you and I know it won't be long until we can hold each other — and just imagine that!

Angelika is very moved as I read back this message: "Will you be including it in the book?" she asks. "Yes," I answer: "We'll continue till it's done." After a moment she adds: "I've been asking your dad to talk to us. I've been telling him how much it is appreciated when he talks to us."

15: A PATTERN OF PERFECTION

May 23

My body and spirits are revived by the beauty of this place. I had a long walk on Carmel beach after lunch, and decided there's no more palpable joy than a pack of dogs playing in the surf. Watching them dash in and out of the waves with boundless energy is a straight shot of ecstasy.

At our appointed time I enter Angelika's room where she is slightly propped up on her bed with the usual assortment of pillows. "Are you ready for me?" I ask. "Yes. Absolutely." We are both looking forward to our regular meditation.

Following a silence that is full of gratitude, I begin to feel Dad's presence:

Angelika: I want to speak with you again about this space. I want you to trust that everything that happens here is perfect. This one is hard for me to describe because it's a new concept, one that hasn't really been introduced there yet. I'll try to give it to Jane in a way she can understand:

"Over-soul" is a pattern of perfection — like a perfect grid, a direct and true alignment. The great enlightened beings of this earth have had direct contact with this alignment.... They've learned skills to effect this order of being — as opposed to a sort-of chaos that is loosely characteristic of the earth-bound vibratory patterns. So it is possible for one person to effect perfection in a vertical sense, by attunement with this over-soul. It's also possible for whole groups to align with pure intention but it doesn't often happen. Here it is the case. And that is a little deeper (though still inept!) explanation of what I meant when I said that everything that is happening here is perfect.

There are other things I want to speak with you about ... physical things, pertaining to the body. I'm going to try....

The body is not a body. That's lesson number one. As you've heard and read in other places, it's a collective mirage. When my body ceased, I was exactly the same Harry Lee Smith, Jr. I was when I went to bed earlier that night (only, as I said, free and refreshed, etc.) I guess I'm telling you what to expect (or not to expect). You will be as you are now. Because now is always. Your being is eternal. Some of the scales will fall from your eyes and you'll experience and learn new and exciting things. But the you who speaks to me and loves me and whom I love: This you is inalterable and continuous.

So be here with me now, and we are in the changeless eternal alignment where all things are possible and where all joy exists. And here words really fail me. It's better if I don't try to describe it. The words only cast shadows on this light I'm holding out for you to see. Close your eyes and grasp it, my love. I am here.

Fire the Rockets

May 24

Our afternoon meditation time arrives, and I find Angelika reading in her room. It always amazes me that while I need to have adventures, write, talk on the phone and move about each day, Angelika is somehow able to remain here in virtually the same position, constantly. She can bristle at small inconveniences, but her usual attitude is one of acceptance.

I make a bit of small talk, reporting on my day, and we begin our shared silence. After several minutes, I feel Dad's presence:

Today is a special day for us ... for you. Think about it. It's a bit of a celebration, so there's a mood of excitement. This is not a lesson day – it's a celebration day. Lighten up! This is joyful: This is good. All the energy is really wonderful. Get up and dance (figuratively speaking!) Play music! Sing! It's a good, really good day. You both look so serious (I was going to say gloomy). Fire the rockets! Sound the trumpets! Rejoice!

I feel quite confused by this — have I somehow lost the scent?

Jane: Something's changing and it's all good. Trust what you don't understand. Angelika's receiving something new. She can hear me. This is wonderful. Ask her!

Angelika: Are you ready? The angels are here: Are you ready?

Still confused, I interrupt the meditation to read what I've recorded and ask Angelika if she has any idea what Dad is talking about. She looks at me blankly and we return to silence. Soon I feel the presence of Spirit:

Harry's excitement is very great.
He is learning things that dazzle him
and give him great hope.
And as he experiences them, he also knows that any moment
they will be shared with Angelika,
and this multiplies his joy.
Sometimes he cannot contain his excitement.

Behold my glory.
Behold my deathless self
bathing each infinite particle of this deathless creation.
Do you want to know the truth?
Nothing here exists but bliss.
Harry gazes at this bliss with the wonder of a
child looking at a gleaming toy, a sparkling, magic, endless gift.
Sometimes he is giddy with excitement.
And why not? He was blind and now sees!
Everything he ever hoped for is real ... beyond his imagining!
His Beloved is alive in his heart, as God-self,
and soon Angelika joins him in this ecstatic union.

My father speaks:
Angelika, this is the excitement I feel and I want you to feel it
with me. It's true. It's all bliss, beyond description. And we're
here together. The mask is falling away and I couldn't be more
excited about this. It's a wild ride, is all I can say. So hold onto
your hat!

It's Really No Great Magic

May 27

Because I am returning home later today, I decide to share meditation time with Angelika in the morning as well as the afternoon. We never know which visit will be our last, and we feel the need to seek wisdom and strength from these invisible helpers who are illuminating the journey.

After we wait together in silence, Dad speaks:

Jane: My purpose now is to envelop Angelika in love energy. This is my focus, so I'm not surprised that she's perceiving some dancing colored light. I'm working pretty hard at this, in a joyful way. I can embody love, you see, in a way that Angelika receives. So it's my love and it's also the Source love — Beloved, as you call it — who is the Light Source. (These things are hard to translate!)

This work is held in perfection, and it will be realized. It is a great work that we three have been allowed to co-create. I am proud of us all. (Three is perfection, you know!) Travel well. Do not worry about anything. Do not let your energy be drained by worrying about Angelika. Believe in these messages, Jane. Believe that I'm as real as I've been in the body, more real. And we found the portal to communicate. It's really no great magic: Such communication is available all over the place. But yes, we are blessed, and you may trust that Angelika is held here in perfect love and care. And the forces that hold her are stronger than anything your earth has to offer.

The mighty force of eternal protection enfolds her now and now and now. By that I mean: Within every possible dimension. It is a strength of protection you cannot grasp.... Only imagine with your heart a great creature of immeasurable proportion who holds her precious child within her grasp with infinite tenderness and fierce and perfect strength. And go in peace, love and joy.

As I am catching an evening flight east, we are able to have a last meditation at the usual time in the afternoon. We wait on Spirit in silence.... Harry speaks:

Angelika, I want to make something clear to you: You have the capability of receiving my thoughts now. As you speak to me and as you rest, please believe and open yourself to the certainty that you hear me. It is not auditory. It will emanate from a sense of presence ... a familiar feeling. Trust the familiar feeling. It isn't lofty, remember, it's really quite ordinary — it is myself as I have lived beside you all these years.

So you have the familiar feeling of me and you open your heart to it, as you are doing, and you trust the little thoughts that come unbidden into your mind. It's already happening, you know. You already do feel my thoughts, and you have repeated them aloud sometimes. So just trust them. When you ask, or when you speak to me, trust that I am answering. It's not so special ... it's really ordinary, in a way. You speak, I listen.... I speak, you listen.... And this way we are even closer in this space. We'll make it easy for you. Whatever else, know I'm here ... always, in every moment. Don't work at it. It simply is: Accept it.

Thank you for taking this journey with me. Thank you for your faithfulness, your humor, your thoughtfulness, your love. I am grateful for you. You have been one of the great lights of my life. I'm so grateful that we have made this journey together. And: I'm grateful that you will soon open to the splendid journey in the Spirit Realm.

Be Tender With the Messenger

May 28 - New Hampshire

Home again, I feel tired, fragile ... as if I have left part of myself behind. I try to journal a bit....

"Dad: I have returned home but feel some sense of being lost and disoriented. It is hard to leave Angelika ... to be back in the web of so much activity when my heart had accustomed itself to simplicity — connecting with Angelika, reading, meditation and inner focus.... Please speak to me."

Jane, the process now is something you must hold within the realm of spirit: That is where we live. You may feel lost for a time as Angelika leaves her body and as our glorious work quiets its energy. Remember, this is also the next phase — equally precious — where you (and we) will hold and publicly share this gift of divine spiritual discourse. You may begin to imagine thirsty and dispirited souls drinking deeply these words of hope, direction and assurance: What a tender gift!

Be tender now with the messenger — my beloved daughter. Be especially gentle and loving with her. Send up that strong spiritual shield against anything that would threaten your inner connection with this beautiful work. Hold it well. "Brood" over this manuscript, like a faithful hen who trusts her eggs will hatch new life. Brood and do not feel the least bit guilty or apologetic. It is now the time to wait on this birthing. The bearing yields fruit ... but it takes time, patience, rest and <u>abundant</u> self-love. I'll be here.

16: FLIMMERING

June 3 - New Hampshire

After several days of gentle rest I have a lovely talk with Angelika this evening. She is excited to tell me about her reading with Delora Ann of Dr. Michael Newton's *Destiny of Souls*. Apparently there are several passages that mirror our messages from Dad. She relates a therapeutic regression with an "advanced soul" who spoke about his sudden death and the great shock and grief of his widow. Apparently, through focused energy signals, he found special ways to assure her of his presence. He discovered that he could send energetic impulses to the spot behind her ear where she liked to be kissed.

Angelika says: "That would mean nothing to me!" She adds that Dad assures her of his presence by sending signals in the form of "flimmerings" in the area where his photos are placed (near the foot of her bed.) "I always knew that's him," she says with great excitement, "but to get a confirmation like that is wonderful."

She cites another passage in which this same advanced soul was asked by Dr. Newton if there would ever be a time — as he progressed along his path — when he would not be in contact with his wife. "Never," was his firm reply: "I will always come to her when I am summoned." These words were almost identical to my father's on March 7.

"I thought you'd like to hear about that," Angelika says, "to reassure you when you begin to doubt these messages." Odd, how lately it is Angelika who is reassuring me....

It seems that she has settled into a sort of routine where she speaks to Dad, then sees the golden and red flimmering in the area around his photos at the foot of the bed. She talks to him, then feels little thoughts or responses: "If I see the flimmering and know he's there it is enough. It makes me happy." I remind her that Dad said this was what he really wanted, for her to know he's there.

It is so comforting for me that she feels she's not alone, even though so much of the time she is physically alone in her room. "I only want to know how soon," she says with some emotion. "Your dad keeps saying, 'Soon.' I wish I knew what that means."

When I voice my concern now about her long wait, she expresses her resolve: "There's no use getting upset." She rests and reads, takes her meals on schedule, visits with Delora Ann, and awaits our phone calls. "From the time I wake up in the morning I look forward to speaking with you."

June 4

In my morning quiet, I'm hoping to have a message for Angelika…. My thoughts drift off, and soon I begin to feel that I am not alone. There is the particular warmth of my father's presence:

Angelika knows I'm with her. That's all I've wanted since I left my body that night. Now she knows, and we confirm it over and over. You'll be amazed when you see what's real. It's almost the opposite of what we're taught to believe in that life: That things you could touch were real and things unseen should be doubted. Actually it's quite the other way around. When you've slipped from the body and the physical world, you don't feel any less real. But the volume gets turned up on inner feelings and spiritual — or etheric — perceptions. Because we realize that what we see and feel with the senses comes from the finer emanation. (We don't have to get too metaphysical here.)

But I want to say that these emanations are also always available to you who are still in mortal body. Because we are in the same place. I believe Angelika is more and more aware of this. If my intention can create these visual signs (flimmerings) and she can recognize them as the form I project to show her I'm here, then there is an intentional source of everything else you see, hear, smell and touch. And that intentional source is the abiding reality. Invisible energy creates the visible world.

We are together increasingly. You can say this in the book. Say that a husband and wife can work side-by-side in the realm of abiding reality even as one has left the physical body and the other remains.... You now know that this is true. And so many others who wish to can find — or rediscover — such partnerships to companion their life and work ... to strengthen their intentions.

The work of weaving energetic power between visible and invisible realms can be immensely creative. To consciously receive guidance from the unseen helpers is a beacon for the mortal traveler. Angelika is acting as a model for how this can be done, even in a state of physical compromise. She has not let her body's limitations confuse her, ultimately. She perceives the true path and possibility of her life's energy. And we together enjoy the sweet partnership that will only expand.

We are both learning about love ... and we are learning it together. What more could I ask for?

God is the Eternal Now

July 13 - Carmel

It is my first full day back here, and I am grateful to return to the singular focus of this amazing journey with Angelika, Dad, and Spirit. Feeling a bit jet-lagged this morning, I try to center myself in silence and receive.... I picture my quieted self leaning against a circumference of being whose center is the throne of God. And I breathe and wait, enjoying the pleasant sensations....

"What do you wish to say to me today?"

We are here. We are delighted to be here with you.
The more you release the illusion of separation,
the greater will be your capacity to feel joy. Joy is everywhere.
Odd, perhaps, to say this as you have been so intimate
with loss in these past months....
But loss is part of the illusion, as you have seen.
For you have heard the voice of joy and hope
in the midst of what appear to be appalling circumstances.
You have seen miracles of light emanating from
apparent darkness. There is no separation from God.
Those who experience the shadows of mortal existence
often also experience the greatest clarity, the brightest light.
Often it is apparent well-being and assurance
that obscure the pathways of divine consciousness.
So do not feel overly troubled by the tragedies of this world,
as every disturbance in this mortal energy
is a divine opportunity.
Behold it in this way and you will wear an inward smile.
Everything is an opportunity for grace.

Do you have a message for Angelika? She seems especially tired, and there are (as predicted) increasing minor but painful complications....

We will be attending you in the afternoon session with Angelika.
It is not your job to know the progress of Angelika's journey.
Your job is to be present to God-self in you. That is all.

In our afternoon session in Angelika's room I tell her of
this morning's message, and she finds the last bit particularly
amusing (about my minding my own business!) We enter into
quiet together.... I feel a warm rush of emotion in my chest as I
receive Dad's presence.

Angelika should be reminded that I am always here. I never
leave her side. I am so grateful that she knows my presence
through the flimmerings and other signs, and I am grateful for
the peace of her resting.

What I and the teachers here are stressing to you now is patient
presence in this moment. It is only in this present moment
that we exist. God is the eternal Now. And only through this
attitude of opening to present moment can we — any of us —
experience divine knowledge or bliss.

It is like a lovely box of sweets that can only be experienced as we
take the time to sit down, open the box, and taste this delicious
treat. It does no good to carry the box around with you, look at
it ... study it. No good to think of it or even plan for or remember
it. Taste it now, and see that it is sweet and delicious.

As a culture, we are very much concerned with productivity, but
we are not good, in general, with the simplest thing: Tasting
the nectar of life in this moment. We live as if there were too
much to do and not enough time. When in fact there is so much
time we cannot even imagine the vastness of it. All time is
ours. And in fact there is not so very much to do. Not really.
Remember when I said that none of the things I worried about
while alive were of any real importance? That is true of most
of the things I did as well.

Angelika exemplifies this truth, for in her stillness I believe she has never been more in touch with what is most important in life. It is a beautiful irony ... and a good example to us all. (Even here many souls haven't lost that imperative of busyness. It's really funny at times, when we look at ourselves and consider that most of this activity is quite useless.)

You can open that box of chocolates any time. Jesus exemplified this great teaching when he said: "Seek first the kingdom of God and all these things shall be given to you as well." The sweet treasure is not only the doorway to present joy and true pleasure, but it is also the doorway to every other gift as well.

I think that is the teaching of today: Everything you seek is here now. Open yourself to it.

I am here. And all my love is here.

As I share this message aloud, Angelika keeps dropping off to sleep, though when I ask if I should stop reading she rouses herself to say: "No: Please go on." Delora Ann says she has been like this for several days.

17: THE HOME STRETCH

July 14 - Carmel

My daughter Susan has phoned to say that Doug's latest MRI reveals a brain tumor. This explains his increasing confusion: He has not been recovering as he should. My heart expands with sadness — for my children, for this Doug who is so vulnerable, so open-hearted. There will be a biopsy, more tests and interventions....

I tell Angelika about these developments when we convene for our afternoon meditation. After a concentrated pause, she reflects: "Maybe it was just for a while..." referring to Doug's return.

We enter into silence. Spirit comes....

We are the continuous explosion of Light,
the explosion that was from the beginning
and is ever expanding, ever radiating.
We burst forth from all things continually.
That is why there can be no death:
All particles are forever radiating light energy,
whether rocks or trees or human souls.
Nothing that is can cease to be.
Its visible form changes,
but the life energy is continuous.
Know that Doug's life energy is continuous.
The opening of his soul to Love will not diminish or die.
The expansion continues ... such is the beauty of creation.
Know this, and do not doubt it —
for this steady knowledge is the foundation of abiding joy.
Messengers of love are everywhere,
allow them to comfort and enliven you.
Receive their ministrations.

"Do you have a message for Angelika today?"

We wish to give to <u>you</u> now, Jane.
We shower your spirit with healing light.
This, to replenish you. Let us restore your spirit.
We are always here with and for Angelika.
We continually radiate divine presence into her being
as she prepares for her journey.
You also need to receive this light. Allow. Rest.

Dad speaks:
Angelika knows that I love her and am always with her. And I want you to know, Jane, that I am here for you, too. I will be looking out for this situation (with Doug) in every way I can, you can be sure of that. It's hard to believe it now, but good will come of this, it always does. That's the gravy. Good always comes. There are so many souls on this side making sure of that. You cannot even imagine what a vast orchestration of loving intention is present here for just such circumstances. Many beings are gathered, because we know that our own joy and health depend upon helping others ... and so we do it in every possible way, with joy and gusto.

That's why I'm saying to you today: Let it come to you. Accept help, grace, nurture. I know it's not an easy reflex for you. With the kind of service work you're doing, you'll need to receive a lot. So try to get used to it. Try to tune into it. It has its own frequency, actually ... not exactly the one you're used to for channeling communications. It's a lovely frequency. Learn to enjoy it. It'll always be available to you in the life you've chosen.

So I'm glad you're here, by Angelika's bedside where so many loving helpers are present. It's a good school for you, too.

As I read the message to Angelika she begins to dip her head in sleep. When I ask if I should continue, she urges me to go on. I ask: "How is this rest?" and she looks satisfied. It's not an empty rest, I gather. And when I try for more detail she answers: "It's hard to describe.... It's a constant thing, and if you have any questions, you ask.... And then the flimmer comes."

"Like a constant communication?" I ask.

"Something like that."

I tell her, "The readers will want to know." She smiles. Then I ask about this process of "allowing" that she has been studying with Delora Ann. She stares with a slight smile at some fixed point in the distance. "Any clues?"

"No. It comes by itself."

"You probably don't like it when I try to pick your brain."

"No. It sort of closes." We laugh.

Blessings on the Just and the Unjust

July 15

I am spending time outside this morning, taking in the beauty of the valley beneath me and the mountains beyond, and trying to flex this new muscle of allowing. But there is inner resistance in aligning with this state, which seems to bring such peace to Angelika. For me, there is a shadow place of discontent — I don't know what it is. Maybe it's shame, or unworthiness. Otherwise, why would I not just lie back, release the controls, and bask in it?

"Dad: How shall I bask in it?"

Begin by understanding that none of us — not one — "deserves" the degree of divine light that is forever flooding us. Truly. And if there were some hierarchy, why is it that God "showers blessings on the just and the unjust?" For that is certainly true: All beings are equally blessed. A criminal of evil intention is no more or less blessed than a flower or a bird ... or a saint. The saint might have more inkling of it, and more gratitude. But divine light is directed everywhere.

When someone receives it, there is a sort of mutual dance that seems to excite and enhance the love energy, a bit like using leaven in the dough. The energy can be encouraged to rise, but it is a very democratic energy that beams on, regardless. A yogi or a saint can indeed magnify this power to perform seemingly superhuman feats or exhibit extraordinary love or charity. That is a wise use of Light. But it all begins with the reception. Energy cannot be directed by or through you if you have not received it for yourself. And at times when you offer it more intensely, you must be more available to receive and recharge. The greater your outpouring, the more deeply you must be filled. Now you are filling up on air and natural beauty. You are breathing these essences. Good work! And again, thank you.

In our afternoon shared meditation, Dad continues his lesson....

As I was saying before, Jane: "Rain falls on the just and the unjust...." The high frequency of pure love energy is always available, but it is the wise person who learns, while on earth, to work with it. This work can take every possible form from poetry to physics to physical healing. Here we work with energy all the time for it is all we have.

I am telling you this because I personally didn't see the importance of trying to work with energy until the past several years. And I wish I had begun it sooner! It doesn't have to be anything fancy — no magic tricks. Just begin by noticing the unseen is the source of everything, and take it from there.

Angelika has found the direct channel for the concentration of light energy that is here in her room, as extra helpers who specialize in transition are assembled ... and you can see how much peace it brings her. What a sad thing that most people pass their days in the sort of activity that might be likened to a hamster on his little treadmill! There is no fruit to this sort of activity, but people don't know how to get off the thing. That's why illness or some other dramatic interruption can be such a gift.

Use your time wisely. Just keep up the good work. Because the real fruit is the joy of being, literally, IN Love. It is the unspeakable blessing of being fully attuned to this light energy which is everywhere available.

A Malignant Tumor

July 17

Today I have learned that Doug's tests show a brain tumor that is aggressive and malignant. My reaction is deep sorrow and frustration. The possibilities are too painful to contemplate. Will they poison this new, loving creature so briefly in our midst with chemo and radiation and ruin the last of his life? I cannot bear the thought. This Doug has a spirit so tender ... and his mind is fragile, his consciousness itself a delicate balance of heart sentiment and disorientation.

Over the phone my dear friend Judy reminds me of all the good that his brief sojourn has brought, all the fruit of these few months since he has returned from "the Other Side." And maybe that is all. Perhaps it's not in his best interest to prolong his life in any way possible.

I'm looking for help from Dad and the other generous spirit helpers who come to me. I don't know much about you ... are you angels? Guides...? You don't speak much about yourselves.

We are here. We are ministering helpers who will always be with you — that is all you need to know.

Please help me with the pain of this situation. And help me to help my children.

Look at the arc of Doug's life. Notice the journey into a place of great restriction ... then look at this near fatal stroke that has given him soul revelation and cleansing. And see that he seized the opportunity — against great obstacles — to redress the errors of his life and above that to spread humor, love, joy, forgiveness.... That is a great arc for one life. A brain can only withstand so much. There may be no more physical miracles for Doug Bernhardt. But the lasting kind, the spiritual and emotional miracles, have abounded in this scenario.

Be grateful, as you observe in awe the blessings one soul has offered when he saw that life is full of love, forgiveness, and infinite possibility. Appreciate what his body endured for these great lessons ... and that he chose to come back and share them before going on to live in the realm of Spirit. Be grateful, and allow stillness and even holiness to replace anxiety ... for there are deep mysteries that surround each mortal life, and we must bow before them, even as we try to see the hand of Spirit behind, before and within all that is briefly visible.

Doug's eternal spirit will return to the place he briefly visited and there he will feel your gratitude and hope for the happiness of his wife and his children. He will be able to have a full heart, knowing that he gave love and healing and hope.

Respect his great effort by not being trapped in the lower vibrations of clinging to what is passing. No regrets, no prolonged sorrow. Because Doug Bernhardt has done a great and heroic work with his heart, mind, body and spirit. And that is the legacy his family and friends can cherish and carry on throughout their lives.

In the afternoon I share this message with Angelika, and after some reflection she says that this will be good for the children to hear — but later, when they are ready to receive it. Then we enter into our own quiet meditation....

I feel warm fullness of light and benevolent, loving presence:

We are here. There is nothing new to report.
As you experience, this room is alight with spiritual presences.
We bless and surround you and Angelika as you meditate.
For both of you we wish that this time together
will be blessed with gratitude and sweetness.
Let it be a joyful time, and do not try too hard for understanding.
Sometimes there are no words.

Be grateful for this peace,
which is not often experienced where you live.
Angelika has entered a world beyond words.
Accept this transition and learn from it.

Our love is with you.

Divine Receptivity

Angelika, honey: Just be patient a little while longer – we're in the home stretch now.

These words come to me as I gaze at the small display of my father's photos that is at the foot of Angelika's bed. I feel Dad's message so tangibly, and repeat his words again: *"We're in the home stretch now."*

"I hope so," Angelika responds. And then she smiles and says: "I see the flimmering."

After lunch I return to join Angelika for our regular time of meditation. I do the usual preparations of turning off the phone's ringer and alerting the care-giver that we'd like to be undisturbed. Then I rearrange her little altar: The fresh flowers flanked by photos of Harry as a young naval officer, Harry as an older man, and the couple together, looking out from a New Year's celebration. Then I assume my usual spot beside her bed, and we wait....

My father speaks:
Angelika: I'm speaking to you and to Jane ... and Spirit Guides are joining me in this message.

You have graciously entered into this sphere of divine receptivity and we are very grateful for your submission and acceptance of this high level of human attainment. What these helpers wish to articulate is a sort of accolade for a level so little understood within our society. And so we are going to elaborate on this, even though you yourself must already know much of what I'm going to convey through Jane.

Human life enjoys many phases, and in this part of the world vast over-emphasis is placed on the phase of material/ physical productivity. That has certainly contributed to our society's wealth and there is nothing wrong with it, as a developmental phase. Alas, appreciation of other levels of human advancement is often obscured by the emphasis placed on material product. And so the abstract thinker, the artist, and the nurturer of other souls are far less valued than is healthy for a balanced and enlightened human system. But perhaps least valued of all is pure receptivity — the great art of allowing oneself to be still and enable other energies to communicate with and fertilize the self.

A flower allows sunlight and rain to help it to grow and radiate beauty ... and then it offers its nectar to insects for pollination. This is a great and beautiful service to the heightened realms of earthly sensitivity.

A tree allows itself to receive light and provide shade; it offers its branches as a home for many other creatures. Indeed, if we look around ourselves, we see that pattern echoed throughout the earth: Self-offering ... patience ... receptivity. Even those creatures whose task it is to move or carry, hunt or gather, are heeding spiritual impulses which guide them in their simple tasks.

In this evolutionary moment, there is no task on earth more imperative than divine receptivity. It involves a revolution of perception. Yet this wisdom is age-old. Jesus said: "Consider the lilies of the field, who neither toil nor spin, yet even Solomon in all his glory was not arrayed as one of these." He meant: Receive. Allow the universe to bless and endow your life as if there were a real and present God whose love is all-powerful and abundant.

Here, in the realm of pure Spirit, we can produce nothing that can be bought or sold. And for some, arrival here can be a rude awakening. "What am I to have and do?" they wonder, feeling a bit lost. Certainly, helpers will guide them. They will not wander aimlessly if they are willing to learn. But why not learn the most precious lessons now? Tune your soul to the frequency of love and enlightenment. Allow silence to blossom into wisdom. Train your heart to receive. How beautiful is the realm that waits to be received by you.

Angelika: I am so grateful that you are embodying now this human station. As I said earlier: It won't be long. I'm here. I love you.

On I Go From Here

July 20

Returning from an afternoon outing in Carmel, I learn that my daughter Susan has tried to call me several times. When we speak she tells me that her father has had another severe brain hemorrhage. This time there will be no reprieve.

I am faced with a difficult choice, but my priority seems clear: I phone the local cab company — with no flight plan, no reservations or agenda — and ask: "How soon can you get me to the airport?" My heart is racing as I pack: Will I be able to reach Doug's bedside to be with our children while he is still alive? The kind young Mexican driver arrives within fifteen minutes, allowing for only a quick farewell to Angelika.

While she understands my need to leave immediately, this timing is wrenching for us both. Once again our visit is cut short: We are not ready to say good-bye. As I embrace her to leave, Angelika focuses her eyes on mine with a look of such intensity it seems to encompass all the space before and after this moment: "Everything will be taken care of," she says, pronouncing the words deliberately — as in, "from now on."

The cab driver sweeps me up and, feeling my anxiety about being able make all the necessary plane connections, he says: "*He'll* make it all work out. You're on a good mission." Amazingly, all the connections work smoothly: Carmel to San Jose, San Jose to Boston…. I couldn't have arranged it more perfectly.

During the last long leg of the journey as I sit stiffly in my airplane seat, I begin to experience again the odd sensation of Doug's thoughts drifting into mine. Without judging whether it is "true" I take up my pen and write:

What has happened to me has been so far beyond anything I could possibly have imagined. First the confusion and terror of it (from which I was protected) then the help from so many people who visited me while I was out of my body. And the other ones which still I don't comprehend — the helpers that knew everything about what I was going through, and what lay beyond. This reality I never really imagined: Love, forgiveness, a clean slate. Wide open freedom to create anything at all in life. At first I felt so bad, so humble, but the mercy! These helpers saying: "Don't go there ... let it go. Try on forgiveness, love, opportunity."

At one point (I don't know exactly when) it wasn't enough to just know this and go on. I really wanted to try to come back and make things right, to share what I found.... I didn't mind at all the cost of it because this is the supreme, continual condition of our lives. I <u>decided</u> to share it because I was so full of the hope and wonder of it.

And I got to do so much. I got to love everyone I really loved but was held back with. I got to give myself and share the glory. Boy, I can't tell you how good that felt, even though there was pain and difficulty. It was the best.

Things are different now. I have a new closeness with all my family. I love them all so much. I'm O.K. to let it go now where I wasn't before. I'm so grateful for the chance to be with you all with all my love, to say the things I needed to say. You were (are) so wonderful to me — every one of you. I appreciated everything.

I hope you can take what I've experienced and tried to share. Let it change your lives for the better. I'm not going anywhere, you just won't see me for a while. This part I don't quite get but I'm on my way, and it's not fearful at all. Believe me — there's no emptiness for me now. Good things are waiting. So you need to feel your feelings but keep looking at the big picture. I got to have this time to really feel and express my love for each one of you. And I hope above anything that you take this and remember it and pass it on. It'll make the world a better place. It certainly changed my world!

It won't help to feel too bad about this. I guess I got a rare chance to come back and fix things. Yeah, I wanted to be there longer as your dad, husband, friend ... but that's not the way it was! I was too shut down! So this is the way I got to be really free of all of that. And I hope you'll come to see it the way I do — as a miraculous opportunity.
On I go from here.
I'll be in touch. I love you all so much.

I arrive in Boston first thing in the morning and am met by my daughter Jessica and her husband, Suresh. We drive directly to the hospital where Doug's wife Ari and his sisters are waiting, along with our children Susan and John. The doctor's latest report is that there will be no reprieve: Doug's unconsciousness is permanent. It is up to Ari to make the decision to remove him from all life support. In a miracle of solidarity we join together in this difficult decision — the in-laws I haven't seen in years, the second wife I hardly know, my children and I ... simply loved-ones vigiling together at a death-bed.

We take turns sitting in Doug's room and traveling the hospital corridors for prayer, a conversation, a cup of tea. There is a sense of immediacy and inevitability: Doug is not expected to be able to breathe for any length of time without support. Sometimes we sing for him, and share remembrances by his bed. At one point when Susan and I are alone with him I read aloud the stirring meditation I received on July 17th after learning of his malignant tumor. Ari enters, apologizing for interrupting, but I offer to read the message to her and she is so moved that she asks if I will read it at Doug's funeral.

Late into the night John and I, exhausted, reluctantly abandon the bedside vigil. I will leave Susan to tell in her own words the last moments with her father in the early morning hours of July twenty-first:

"In the quiet of your room, we all snuggled in around you.

White noise, machines, small souls wrapped in white blankets and in the warmth of your presence.

We waited. We accepted. We listened to you breathe. We dreamt strange dreams of struggle and confusion. We woke to find you passing. We huddled and encircled you.

And helped you breathe.

We told you our truth and you looked upon us with your last breath.

What a precious gift.

How can so much beauty be in one small moment. You followed us home in the bluest sky, smattered with clouds. Over the bridge. And the sky was so vast....

I see you in the sky, smell you in the grass, feel your warmth from the sun on the backs of my sleepy legs. You are with me, all around me, and it is so beautiful. I cherish this moment ...

Don't let me forget that fleeting moment of life into death.

Life into life.

You saw me.

Wind in my hair, carried me home. I close my eyes and feel you all around me.

So much beauty, I cry ... tears of joy.

Thank you for this beautiful day. This beautiful life. Thank you for a beautiful man.

Arm in arm, cheek to chest, hand in hand.

You are my heart.

You are my angel.

White noise.

Breathe in and out. Lull me to sleep.

It won't be long now.... It's time.

No more pain, only peace.

You didn't leave us in the night, in the struggle. Not until we were peaceful. With you.

'I love you, everything will be okay, you did such a good job.'

Thank you for giving us that precious moment.
For allowing us to see your spirit.
Infinite love ... infinite possibility....
A blank check.
All of our children together...
What a beautiful day.
Most beautiful Sky."

18: THE END

Six days pass and I am standing in the church in Massachusetts where Doug and I were married, preparing to deliver a powerful message of forgiveness to a sanctuary crowded with friends and family. The service is magnificent, containing all the elements Doug loved — rousing hymns, praise music, funny and moving stories, the Eucharist. We all feel his spirit as a friend sings one of the beautiful songs he wrote: "Thank You for Your Calling." Both John and Jessica climb the pulpit to tell the amazing story of their reconciliation with Doug.

Later, John would write:
"I will always be grateful for the brief time he was able to come back to us. For the burden he helped me to shed. The love that he spread was unmistakable. Anyone who was around him was made better by his constant mood and demeanor of kindness and genuine thankfulness to just be alive. What a simple concept that seems lost in our everyday society. Life IS truly a gift and no one knew that better than he.

What exactly he saw and experienced on the other side I suppose I will learn in time. But for him it was profound and monumental beyond any life experience I have witnessed.

As I write this I feel what still comforts me more than anything is the thought of him happy. I KNOW he is in a better place filled with love and happiness and a sense of common purpose beyond measure. I have never been one to put much stock in spirituality and life after death. As much as I feel I have an open mind, I find now that I still have worlds to learn.

My father was singularly instrumental in opening my eyes to a world beyond my own. Much like a child gazing at a million stars for the first time, I now know there are things beyond sight, sound and touch. Overwhelming as the vastness of it all is, my father had always taught me to take things in stride. Why should this be any different? We don't have to figure it out all at once. In a world that moves with the speed of a jet, sometimes the simplest explanations can be found in the warmth and simple solitude of peaceful thought.

My eyes and ears are now open to whatever awaits me. With open arms I accept the things I do not know, cherish those I do and wonder about the unknown.

Thank you, Dad."

Exhausted after the service, Jessica and I are slumped into a couch in the church hall long after the rest of the guests have gone when the receptionist finds us to say we've had a phone call from my sister, Carol.

Angelika has died.

Apparently she left her body sometime during Doug's funeral. We take a collective breath and try to absorb this news. At what moment did this occur? Perhaps it was exactly as I was reading to the congregation my meditation about Doug, or during John or Jessica's stirring words ... or perhaps we were singing, "Alleluia, He is coming ... Alleluia He is here...."

Stunned that all of this has transpired at once, we meet up with John and Susan at Ari's home, then drive to Carol's house nearby where we light a candle before a lovely photo of Angelika and Dad.

After sitting for a few moments in silence, Jessica and I simultaneously notice that in the photo Angelika's expression seems to have changed: She is smiling now.

July 26

I can't really begin to speak about the intensity of these days, culminating in Doug's funeral and Angelika's death. How do I speak of these things? An amazing, transcendent service ... and in the midst of it, on the opposite coast, Angelika's passing. At 11:35 Eastern time. As predicted, there was a momentary physical emergency of some sort ... and then she was gone. So quickly, her care-giver said. She had her breakfast, called for help, and moments later she was gone.

Can I be sad? How can I grieve? She has said, "How soon is soon?" for almost nine months. And now we know. But in these last weeks she was already there. She was already more with Dad and Spirit than with those of us who passed in and out of her room. She'd drift off, gazing at some spot a few feet away, peacefully.

July 30

In the end, Angelika had passed right by me. I could sit and offer my meditations, beautiful as they were, but she was already in a place more sublime than any my words could summon. And I would watch her eyes go to that other place, then softly close and I would not know if she was sleeping or awake. "She was at peace," is what the care-givers all said. "Peace" being the word we use to summon the ineffable: She had succumbed to mystery. The invisible Lover was her companion at the end.

I wondered about the timing of her death, in the midst of the beautiful service for Doug Bernhardt, who had miraculously emerged from a coma to bring a few months of the purest seeds of love, forgiveness and hope. Could it be that Angelika and her host of helpers used that portal ... that parting of the veil?

I hope for some message now in the drop down days of utter loss and sorrow that follow the great public expression of the ceremonies. Alone now, I cannot imagine comfort for the empty place. In spite of all these spiritual teachings, I feel utterly empty and alone.

We are here.
You are never alone.
We hold with you these mysteries.

We are asking you to rest now from this intense labor.
You have carried your children
through the dying of their father.
You have held a fragile and grieving widow in the embrace
of spiritual truth and love for these nine months,
preparing her for a journey that has been accomplished
with utmost grace and joy.
You have borne these things in your body.
And you have celebrated their joys and endured their grief.
Grief and joy.
There is no more to be done in this moment.
Please know that we are here.
We, Love's angelic messengers, are always here.

September 11

My chest complications have returned, preventing me from accompanying my sisters on their trip to Carmel to begin the massive sorting and clearing of the Smith household. My grief is magnified today: I'm holding so much that cannot be expressed. I loved my dad so much. In a way I really got to have him back in this intense period following his return to spirit, his death. And now he is again distant. Our intimate journey has ended and the veil between us seems more real.

In my journal I write: "Oh, Dad: I have not heard you in so long. In my weakness, I also have not listened or asked for messages. I have been resting. But the mounting inner unrest calls to you and to Spirit: Help me, please, you beings who are unseen but who promise you are here...."

Spirit answers:
We are here. We are here in your resting
and in your waiting.

We are here in patient silence,
loving you deeply as you grieve.

"Dad: Will you speak to me?"

Jane: Angelika and I are together now. I cannot describe to
you the joy we feel. I have been waiting to share with you my
gratitude for all the love and tender care you gave to Angelika
and all the comfort you brought to me. How can I shape words
which will express my gratitude? You were there unfailingly
to help us be together even though separated by my body's
death. I asked and you gave so much of yourself. It was never
my intention to tire you. And we are sorry that you are so
tired and upset. We wish to share with you our joy, as you
have shared so much with us. We are here, Jane, in this very
room where you are crying alone, and watching the rain....
We are here.

I ask for a sign. Minutes later, the phone rings and the
caller ID shows my father's name. It's my sister Susie, calling
from California with an update from the interviews with
realtors at the house. Well, it's *sort of* a sign....

It's the best we could do on short notice, Jane. We'll keep trying.
And you keep resting. This is a time of great receptivity. Much
information is being processed and assimilated, and your spirit-
mind is opening wider to accommodate all that has transpired
in these months. Your tears grease the wheels of this process,
and they also enable the opening of your heart, which is the
seat of spirit-mind.

We have never left you alone, Jane. Many beings are present at
all times to help you in this great work you have undertaken.
You now know that service to one's fellows is God's work, and
you will be richly, even fiercely blessed.

*Odd to say, but now your heart cannot fully accept such bless-
ings. It must slowly accustom itself to much wider receptivity.
To probe this heart too soon is akin to rooting into the frozen
ground of early spring to find a flower before its time. Do you
see? The flower will bloom best if undisturbed. We must wait
for it, watch for it ... know it will come, and find comfort in that
assurance.*

*Trust this unfolding, Jane ... just as you have grown to trust
the messages would come for Angelika. They will come for
you. We are here for you. We serve you, just as you have
served us. With deepest, everlasting gratitude. With you we
await the bloom.*

The Empty House

September 23 - Carmel

My sisters have done an incredible job of sorting and clearing the Smith house. There is a kind of gentleness in the empty spaces. I am sitting on the solitary bed in Angelika's now barren, sun-drenched room. In this spot she waited for nine months for the mystery which has taken place without me. She is gone and I am here in the empty room. I open my journal and write:

"Angelika: I miss you so much. I have loved our time together far beyond anything I could ever have imagined. We held and blessed each other and this part of me that held you is raw and misses you."

Cleared of all its boxes and relics, this is a sunny room. At first I wept when I sat down here ... but now I feel quieted. The view from the bed, revealed after weeks of sorting, is beautiful — a lovely magnolia in the foreground, fir trees in the distance silhouetted against the mountains....

Yesterday's reception "For the Friends of Harry and Angelika Smith" was quite wonderful. Perfect, actually. My sister Susie and I formed a circle of chairs in a bright reception room at the community clubhouse, and we welcomed guests to a space of celebration and remembrance, with photos of the couple, some of their treasures, and light refreshments. All were so grateful as we took turns telling the stories — touching and funny and real. Those who had gathered loved seeing all the photos giving a fuller history of friends they hadn't known in their youthful beauty. Indeed, it is a glorious thing for Harry and Angelika to be united again in the same form. We are the ones who need comfort and encouragement.

September 24

Here in my father's room for perhaps the final time, I have spent a long morning seeking guidance. The sense of losing spiritual partnership with both my father and Angelika since her death has left me somewhat bereft and I have longed for a message.... At last, as I have been re-reading this manuscript, I have begun to feel Dad and Angelika not only present but also deeply with me in love, holding with me the work of this book which is also and equally *their* work: They are actively invested in this. I am assured that whenever anyone opens a copy of this book and accepts its message, they also will receive the loving spiritual presence of Harry and Angelika, and that is the blessing they intend for their readers.

You who have read these words: Please know that they have come from the deepest loving intention of beings in the spiritual realms as well as Harry and Angelika ... May they light your path and enter your heart. You are loved. You are not alone. We are here.

One Last Message

May 23, 2008 - New Hampshire

During my regular quiet time I discover a beautiful journal I gave to my father nearly twenty years ago, in the tentative early years of sharing our spiritual paths. On the inside cover I had written, "For Dad: To record the exciting developments of your spiritual journey." It touches me to read in its pages his earnest desire to improve family relationships as well as his deep dedication to his spiritual progress. Minutes after closing the book I begin to feel — or hear — his voice, and so I take up the pen....

Trust everything that's happened. Before my death we were close in our communication of our spiritual progress. Our conversations were precious to both of us. Angelika also respected your journey into divine communication. So it was easy for us to begin our three-way conversation. The respect was already there. The groundwork was laid. We never doubted the divine meditations you sent. I was very impressed with your progress along the spiritual path, which had taken me so long. I knew that you were on the right track.

Did I expect things to unfold the way they did? Of course not! I never expected to leave Angelika that way. But how perfectly it has all turned out! Look at this sequence of events: You were there for her right away with my words and your spiritual guidance, and she was able to learn and be prepared for her transition out of the body. You grew and learned so much. And now there is a book which will inspire and comfort so many people, Jane. This I am asking you to believe. Fiercely hold this vision that many, many hearts will open like flowers to these words. Then it will grow. People will be asking for more copies and you will take the necessary steps. You don't need to see too far down the road today, but trust this thing, Jane.

I promise you that our book will find its audience. It's out of your hands. As with the early days when you began to receive messages for Angelika, this will be taken care of and you can be a faithful passenger on the trip. Don't worry about anything. Lots of us are moving this thing along, because this is good and important information for the world to receive. Hearts are hungry for these truths.

Enjoy yourself. That's what I always want to see as your dad. The rest will come. Thank you for everything. Never forget how grateful I am. We are always connected, and I rejoice in that. As you can see from my journal, it's what I wanted. So many prayers are being answered.

Love yourself, Jane, just as you are. I'm afraid I missed that step. Just as you are, warts and all. Love, Love, Love. It's the whole truth in a nutshell. There's really nothing else to know in this life. Love is everywhere, all the time … all forgiving, all healing, all powerful. Everything is made up of this energy. Everything. Let it be bed-rock in your life, starting with self-love. I'll be here to help.

Good to be with you. Good to speak with you. On you go from here — new projects, new dreams. This book will find its way.

POSTSCRIPT

March 19, 2009

Yesterday my husband Paul (we were married in May of last year) left this highlighted article on the kitchen island:

France: $1.4 Million Prize for Physicist

Bernard d'Espagnat, 87, a French physicist and philosopher of science, has won the $1.4 million Templeton Prize for his work on the philosophical implications of quantum mechanics, the John Templeton Foundation said Monday in Paris. Noting that the rules governing the behavior of subatomic particles contravene common-sense notions of reality, Dr. d'Espagnat, a professor emeritus at the University of Paris-Sud, coined the term "veiled reality" to describe a world beyond appearances, which science can only glimpse and which he said could only be compatible with "higher forms of spirituality."

New York Times March 17, 2009

We know this now. It is part of our family vocabulary: "Remember when my father said ...? What was it that Doug said about...?" We remind each other of these beautiful revelations. It isn't that uncertainty and grief are gone — not by a long shot — but we have these tokens from the other side of death to remind us that hope, love and joy are the abiding realities.

I need to return to stillness often to regain my center when the concerns of each day begin to dominate and overwhelm my consciousness. But I have increased confidence that unseen spiritual helpers will speak. I haven't heard from my father or Doug in a long time. I've learned from other teachers that for the most part these communications are not easily orchestrated from either side of the veil. Both my father and Doug had goals which they accomplished with purpose and grace.

For me the assurance that spiritual guidance is available to any of us at any time is the lasting lesson. And this I offer to you, the reader. Let this story be one more piece of evidence to confirm the secret hope we all cherish that we are immortal souls here in Earth School who are surrounded by a host of loving unseen helpers available at all times to comfort and assist us. We have only to ask, wait and receive.

All blessings to you,
Jane Smith Bernhardt

About the Author

Photograph by John Hession

JANE SMITH BERNHARDT comes from a family of artists. It was through portraiture that she began to explore art as a medium of social transformation, traveling to the Soviet Union during the Cold War to render charcoal sketches of "enemy" faces. In the decades that followed, she developed three more thematic portrait collections which were exhibited throughout the United States as well as in India, Japan and the UK. As a writer and professional actress, she has also created and performed five dramatic pieces, including *Julia Ward Howe: Crusader for World Peace* and *The Hibakusha Peace Project*. In places as diverse as Auschwitz and Hiroshima, her passion has been to embrace the gifts of darkness and invite the healing light to awaken our hearts to the possibility of a loving global consciousness. She travels widely with her exhibits, performances, lectures and workshops.

Years of training in spiritual guidance, meditation and energy healing have prepared Jane for this journey into the mystery of death itself, which awakens both our greatest fears and our most inspiring possibilities. *WE ARE HERE: Love Never Dies* is her first book. Her website is: www.janebernhardt.com.

Breinigsville, PA USA
12 April 2010
235981BV00002B/2/P